Simply
WINE

Simply
WINE

How to Choose
Good-Value Wines
to Enjoy Every Day

**HEIDI
YORKSHIRE**

Duplex Media Group
Portland, Oregon

Simply Wine
How to Choose Good-Value Wines to Enjoy Every Day

All inquiries should be addressed to:
Duplex Media Group
P.O. Box 12081
Portland, Oregon 97212-0081
503-335-3155

All photography by John A. Rizzo, Rizzo Studio, Portland, Oregon
Design and illustrations by Linda Wisner, Wisner Associates, Portland, Oregon

Library of Congress Catalog Card Number: 99-90299

Library of Congress Cataloging-in-Publication Data:

Yorkshire, Heidi, 1952-
        Simply wine: how to choose good-value wines to enjoy every day / by Heidi Yorkshire.
                p. : ill. ; cm.
        Includes bibliographical references and index.
        ISBN 1-883970-99-7
1. Wine and wine making. I. Title.
TP548.Y   1999
641.2'2—dc20   99-90299 CIP

ISBN 1-883970-99-7

To Joseph

Contents

Chapter 1

The Simplest Thing in the World

In which Sir Winston Churchill provides a role model

ine is the simplest thing in the world.

Walking through a modern winery, all stainless steel, computers and concrete, it's hard to remember that in the beginning wine made itself. Grapes ferment, with or without our help. Archaeologists found ancient traces of wine in northern Iran, in a pottery jar dated around 5000 B.C. That means wine has been part of the human experience for at least 7,000 years.

Put that way it sounds simple enough, yet to many people a bottle of wine contains more uncertainty than pleasure. When they stand in a wine shop or look at a wine list, only questions come to mind: What's the right wine? How much should it cost? Which foods can I serve it with? Will my friends think it's sophisticated enough? Will I like it?

I can't blame anyone for worrying. Wine can be simple, but it's also complicated. Even a typical supermarket carries hundreds of labels. Wines come from familiar places like California and France and unfamiliar ones like Argentina, South Africa and New Zealand. Labels, even when they're in a language you think you understand, use words like "malolactic fermentation" and "sur lie aging." Some bottles cost $5, some cost $50, some you can't buy unless you're willing to pay thousands.

Wine plays many roles, as beverage, commodity, inspiration to poets, intoxicant, social lubricant, agricultural product, status symbol. It's also a work of art. Like other arts, you can approach it many ways and find some satisfaction in any of them.

Take going to the theatre, for instance. Most people don't read a play in advance or spend a lot of time wondering where the actors were trained. Few care whether the director is a friend of the playwright or

God loves fermentation just as dearly as he loves vegetation.
– Ralph Waldo Emerson

whether the lighting designer used pink gels or amber ones. That may be interesting to a serious theater buff, but not to most of us. Instead, we appreciate the experience for what it offers in the moment and for the new perspectives on life that fine art can bring. If a performance is particularly inspiring, we may look back on it with gratitude.

There are three types of wine in the world:
1. I like it,
2. I don't like it, and
3. I'll drink it if someone else is paying for it.

The same is true of wine. What's important is not how much you know but whether you have the level of knowledge that lets you enjoy walking into a wine shop, or drinking wine with friends at a meal. There's certainly no point in agonizing over how much you *don't* know. Sometimes people just can't pour a glass of wine without saying (or thinking) things like: "I'm not a connoisseur. I don't really know what I'm doing. This is just a cheap wine I picked up. My dentist said I should try this. I'm sorry I don't have something better." One comment I hear a lot, no doubt because I write about wine for a living, is, "I like this but *you* probably won't."

In writing *Simply Wine*, my goal is to lessen the anxiety and establish a foundation on which you can build a lifelong appreciation for wine. Wine's pleasures are not reserved for the rich or the ridiculously reverent. The book includes lots of practical advice and debunks some myths that worry neophytes but don't matter at all to wine professionals. It takes the mystery out of some apparently complex aspects of wine, like prices, labels and shopping, and introduces you to some of the *real* mysteries, especially the mystery of place, that make wine a lifelong joy.

Myth #1: price equals quality

Much of the anxiety about wine is caused by price. How can price tags vary so greatly on practically identical liquids sold in similar packages that, truth be told, seem to taste pretty much the same to everyone except specially trained experts? Some folks are convinced that expensive wines taste better than inexpensive wines. Others think that spending more than $10 on a bottle of wine is like throwing money into a dumpster.

In fact, many costly wines have distinctive or unusual flavors that don't please everyone. For the average person, a wine's value is determined by the pleasure it brings, not its scarcity or renown. It doesn't matter how much you paid for a wine if you don't enjoy it. Paying $10 for a wine you don't like is a waste of money. Paying $35 for a wine you don't like is a bigger waste of money. The question to ask about any wine is not "How much does it cost?" but "Do I like it?"

Wine prices, like any others, are determined by supply and demand. The rarer and more sought-after the wine, the more it costs. An expensive wine always has one or more of the following attributes. It is: quite old, from a tiny vineyard, made by a celebrated winemaker, from a year with unusually good weather, made using very expensive or time-consuming techniques or praised highly by wine critics.

In general, different wines are suited to different situations, just like clothes. If you're attending the Academy Awards, an Armani tuxedo is just the thing. If you're going to a picnic, Gap khakis are more like it. If you're planning an elegant meal, a rare, old bottle of wine might be appropriate, but with Auntie Emilia's spaghetti bolognese, a robust $7 red from southern Italy will be a far better fit.

If you get very interested in wine, you may want to venture into the wine equivalent of tuxedo territory. For everyday drinking, however, you'll be happier when you learn to pick the best of the many good-tasting, reasonably priced wines that fill the supermarket shelves.

No apologies necessary

Listen up, folks: If you like a wine, you don't ever have to apologize for drinking it, whether it comes from a five liter box or a bottle encrusted with the dust of time. Graham Kerr once told me a story that makes the point perfectly. In 1958, long before Kerr became famous as TV's Galloping Gourmet, he managed Gravetye Manor, a restaurant which had one of England's best and most extensive wine cellars.

One day Sir Winston Churchill, whose taste in wine was legendary, appeared at the door. Kerr showed Sir Winston to a table and handed him the huge wine list – 680 labels.

Churchill flipped through the list as Kerr stood anxiously by. Would Britain's eminent statesman choose a fine Champagne like the Pol Roger he was famous for drinking? Would he order a vintage Sauternes, a rare Burgundy, a century-old Madiera?

It seemed to take forever, but at last Churchill snapped the cover shut. Then, one of the most inspired orators of the century peered at Kerr and said, "Bring me something in the largest possible bottle with the greatest alcoholic content at the lowest conceivable price."

In water, one sees one's own face, but in wine one sees the heart of another.
  – French proverb

3

No apologies from ol' Winnie, no sir. Churchill asked for a wine that would please him, which is what it's all about.

Good wine makes meals more delicious and inspires conversation and camaraderie. It's not an investment. It's not an excuse for boring your friends with a lecture on geology or chemistry. It's not a way to prove you're superior to someone else. It certainly shouldn't be propped up on any pedestal. Yes, wine's complex, but real aficionados let the complexity lead them back to the simple pleasures.

Duke Ellington once said of music, "If it sounds good, it *is* good." I would say the same for wine: If it *tastes* good, it *is* good.

Wine pros are your friends

Information about wine changes constantly. Staying even somewhat up-to-date on regions, wineries, vintages and what-all can consume a vast amount of time. Now I don't know about you, but I've already got a life, and it doesn't allow time for stuffing my brain with information I'll rarely use. For example, on an average day, I don't really care whether the 1995 vintage in the Rheingau region of Germany was good or bad. But if I'm in the mood for a nice, crisp German riesling, and see a 1995 from the Rheingau in a wine shop, how will I decide if I want to buy it?

Simple solution: I'll ask someone who knows more about it than I do. There's no easier way to get a handle on the vastness of wine than to seek the help of wine specialists, in restaurants or retail stores. If you don't take tips from the pros, you won't ever be guided to anything new and will be stuck drinking the same wines forever. (For more, see Chapter 6, A Wine Merchant of One's Own.)

Chapter 2

How to Taste Wine

*In which you learn to taste wine like a pro,
and spit with abandon*

*N*obody is born knowing how to taste wine. We all can *drink* wine. But tasting is a skill you learn, just as you learn to dance, play tennis or roll out a flaky pie crust. In this chapter you'll learn the simple procedure that professionals use for tasting. It's a basic, easy-to-remember drill which focuses the mind on the experience of the senses.

A big part of the fun of tasting is sharing the wines with friends and talking over your impressions. While words can barely approximate a complex sensual experience like drinking wine, you'll find that trying to articulate your impressions will help you remember the wines you've tasted. As each wine goes into your mental Rolodex, so to speak, your repertoire of tastes, aromas, wineries and regions expands. Every time you shop for wine or read a wine list those memories will help you make your selection.

Don't worry about being thought a snob for paying attention to the wine you drink. No one would think you odd if you took the time to smell a steaming blackberry pie fresh out of the oven, or paused to stick your nose in a dewy, apricot-colored rose. Unless you want others to tell you what to drink all your life, you'll need to develop the ability to taste. It's easy, and practicing's a pleasure.

*Over a bottle of
wine, many a
friend is found.*
– Jewish proverb

Begin with your eyes

The main purposes of looking carefully at a wine are to please your sense of sight and prepare you for the enjoyment to come.

Pour an ounce or two of wine into a clear wine glass, preferably one with a good-sized bowl (at least 8 ounces) and a rim that curves inward slightly at the top.

Look at the wine's color against a white background, or hold the glass up to the light. (A white tablecloth is ideal, but you can also simply hold up a piece of white paper behind the glass.) Wines come in many colors, from pale straw to deep, almost opaque purple-black. Very young white wines, less than a year old, often have greenish glints. Some reds, especially those that have been in the bottle for just a year or two, are bright ruby or purple, sometimes with a shocking pink rim.

On the infrequent occasion when something may be wrong with the wine, color can alert you. The color of young white wines may vary from almost clear to golden, but shouldn't be brownish, even on the edges; young reds should have fairly vibrant purple or ruby colors, and should not look brick or brown. Browning may be a sign of heat damage or poor storage conditions. Cloudiness or streaks, signs of spoilage, are very rarely seen today.

The nose is next

The next step in tasting is the most important of all three: savoring the wine's aroma.

What most people call taste is actually a combination of several different physiological functions. The taste buds themselves sense only four basic tastes – sweet, salty, bitter and acid. These form the foundation of the tasting experience, but certainly don't provide enough information to convey the complexity of a wine. (Other nerve endings in the mouth provide the brain with information about the temperature and texture of foods and beverages.)

You perceive the nuances of wine via your sense of smell, which is the true source of at least 80 percent of taste. The aromatic elements of wine are its *esters*, which are compounds of aromatic acids and alcohol. Alcohol evaporates almost immediately when exposed to oxygen – think of how fast you feel a cooling sensation when you dab alcohol on your skin. When the

If you aren't getting much aroma from a wine, there are several possible explanations. 1) The wine's too cold. This is usually a problem with white wine straight from the refrigerator. Let it warm up a bit. 2) The wine's too warm, which you can tell if you're smelling alcohol fumes rather than fruit. This is often true of red wines. Toss the bottle into the fridge for 15 minutes. 3) The wine is simply not very aromatic. Some poorly made wines just don't have much aroma. 4) The wine is spoiled. What you smell is dull and flat, sometimes with a mildew or sherry-like odor. Cork the bottle and take it back to where you bought it.

wine's alcohol evaporates on exposure to oxygen, its esters are released into the air and can then be smelled.

Now, pick up the glass and smell the wine. You should smell a perfectly pleasant aroma, though it may be faint. When wine sits quietly in a glass, its interaction with oxygen is minimal, and the aroma is minimal as well.

Next, put the glass back down on the table and swirl it vigorously. To avoid disaster, your glass should be less than half-full of wine. Swirl by holding the glass by the base and moving your hand as if you're drawing tiny circles on the tabletop. When you've got a whirlpool going, bring the glass to your nose or, if you're wearing nice clothes, bring your nose down to the glass. Inhale deeply. Most people find that the wine smells much more intense. Swirling mixes the wine with oxygen, and the esters get thrilled and just can't contain themselves.

Writer J.M. Scott describes world-class swirling and sniffing perfectly in his 1950 book, *Vineyards of France*. "It is most impressive if you can learn – with a glass of water in your bedroom – to make the wine swish round just below the rim, as fast as a motorcyclist on the wall of death," he writes. "Immediately afterwards cup your two hands around the bowl and bury your nose in it as if you were inhaling something for a cold."

Enjoy the aroma. If you're inclined to analyze, you could talk about which of three general categories the aroma belongs in: fruit (anything from grapes or lemons to mangoes or black cherries); earth (a broad category of aromas including flint, chalk or gravel, and rich scents like humus, fresh mud or mushrooms); or wood (aging in oak barrels can add scents like toast, smoke, vanilla, coconut, cinnamon or clove). Most young wines smell primarily like fruit.

Sensory researchers have been squabbling during the last few years over the existence of a fifth taste, called umami (oo-MAH-mee). *First identified by scientists in Japan almost a century ago, umami is usually associated with saltiness, but it's considered a distinct taste in itself, a kind of "savory" flavor. Foods like mushrooms, cured meats, dried tomatoes and soy sauce are considered rich in umami. You can try to taste umami for yourself by stirring about 1/4 teaspoon monosodium glutamate (MSG) into a cup of warm water. Taste and spit.*

Magazine reviewers love to describe wines with lists of adjectives: green apples, chocolate, black cherry, rubber, ripe apricots, kerosene, roasted hazelnuts, burnt toast and leather, for instance. Sometimes such aromas are subtle, and sometimes they practically jump out of the glass and into your nose. Although this sort of description seems like gospel truth in a magazine, it's really just one person's perception. Differences in physiology, cultural background and life experience mean that different people often smell entirely different things in the same wine.

Surprisingly, your sense of smell can sometimes detect aspects of wine that you would think could only be sensed in the mouth. When a wine has a high acidity level, smelling it can make your mouth start to water, especially along the sides and front of your tongue. When smelling wines high in alcohol, some tasters get a warm, Vaporub-like feeling in the upper chest.

By the way, you're also entitled to say absolutely nothing during wine tastings, which will make people think you're very deep.

Smell is of all senses by far the most evocative: perhaps because we have no vocabulary for it – nothing but a few poverty-stricken approximations to describe the whole vast complexity of odour – and therefore the scent, unnamed and unnamable, remains pure of association; it cannot be called upon again and again, and blunted, by the use of a word; and so it strikes afresh every time, bringing with it all the circumstances of its first perception. This is particularly true when a considerable period of time has elapsed.
– Patrick O'Brian, *Post Captain*

Why red wine is not white wine

Before we move on to the last step in wine tasting, let's take a quick look at where the flavors and aromas in wine come from.

Color is the most easily visible distinction between wines. It's also a key to understanding many invisible – but tastable – distinctions among wines. Wine color is an indicator of everything that comes *along with* the color and creates the differences in the wine's body, aroma and flavor.

As grapes, like most other fruits, ripen, their color deepens. The color makes ripe fruit more attractive and indicates that it's becoming sweeter and less acidic. Imagine the pale, greenish color and sour taste of an unripe peach and you'll understand what I mean. A week or two later, when that peach is perfectly ripened by the sun, you'll taste more than simple sugary sweetness when you bite into it. The warmth of the sun adds layers of complexity to the flavors of the fruit.

Wine grapes are the same. As they ripen, they develop more complex flavors, which are concentrated in the skins and the outermost layers of the flesh of the grapes. These flavors come from a group of chemicals called *phenolic* (fen-NAH-lick) *compounds* which also contain pigments and tannin. A little tannin gives a red wine a nice texture, but too much tannin can make it astringent and bitter.

When grapes are picked and crushed, the *must* – a slush of unfermented juice, grape pulp, seeds and skins – is almost colorless. The longer the skins remain in the must, the deeper the color becomes. The type of wine being made determines when the skins are removed from the must. Most white wines are made from grapes that have yellow or green skins, so skin color itself is not a big issue. However, if a white wine is to be made from red grapes – like the sparkling wines which are made from pinot noir – the skins have to be removed quickly, or the wine will pick up too much color.

If the wine being made is red, the grapes used will be red or purple, and the skins will remain in the must during fermentation. The temperature of the fermenting wine – it usually rises to at least 80 degrees, and often higher – helps extract phenolic compounds from the skins. A number of different techniques used before, during and after fermentation enhance the color and flavor of red wines.

Oak aging: what's the fuss?

Wood barrels of various sorts and sizes have been used for storing and transporting wine since the Iron Age, but it's only in the last few decades of the twentieth century that barrel-aging wine has become a controversial topic. Winemakers today use oak barrels almost exclusively.

In terms of its effects on wine, a barrel is like a tea bag. The first time you use a tea bag, you can make a very strong cup of tea. The second time, you'll get a weaker cup of tea. By the third time, the water in the cup may not even change color. When wine is aged in a new barrel, the effects can be dramatic. The second year a barrel is used, its effect on wine is much less pronounced. By about the third year, there's little effect at all, and the barrel is just a neutral vessel.

When aged in new oak, wine absorbs strong, sweet aromas like vanilla, clove, coconut and caramel. If the interior of a barrel is toasted

You may have heard talk about letting wine "breathe," which means pulling the cork a few minutes or hours before it is served. However, when a bottle is full only a tiny amount of wine is exposed to oxygen through that skinny little neck. Pouring and swirling are far more efficient ways to bring oxygen to the wine and release its aromas and flavors.

over an open flame (winemakers custom-order barrels with light, medium, or heavy toast), smoky and toasty aromas mix in. The longer the wine is left in the barrel, the more oak aromas it picks up. It also picks up body-enhancing tannin, which is especially noticeable in white wines, because they don't have much tannin otherwise.

Used judiciously, oak aging enhances the flavor and complexity of a wine. However, some winemakers, especially in the New World, use so much oak that it overpowers the taste of the grape. Many people love the cookies-in-the-oven aromas of oak aging so much that they don't care whether they can taste fruit. For myself, I go along with pioneering California vintner Louis Martini, who supposedly said, "If I want to taste wood, I'll bite a tree."

Back to tasting: the mouth

Take a sip of the wine. Slurp in a little air, so that the oxygen can again release the flavors and aromas. Move the wine around in your mouth, making sure it gets to every nook and cranny. The pros make odd gargling noises and look like they're chewing the wine. Hold it in your mouth for a few more seconds. Swallow or spit.

Sometimes a wine is so powerful that you can decide thumbs-up or thumbs-down almost immediately. More often, coming to a conclusion takes a little time. Due to the effects of oxygen, a wine can change dramatically within even a few minutes of being poured, and can continue to change for hours. Some wines smell like burnt matches at first, but with a little swirling, that aroma will disappear.

An excellent way to experience the basic tastes of wine is to do the Tea Tasting, page 109. It will give you a good foundation for further tasting.

Start by tuning in on the bigger things and working toward the smaller ones. Ask yourself some questions. How does the wine *feel* in your mouth? Hearty, delicate, full-bodied, light-bodied, firm, cushy? Is it smooth, silky, velvety, rich, thin or zesty? Does acidity make it feel sharp, or a lack of acidity make it feel flabby and lifeless?

Some red wines are high in tannin, a compound found in grape skins and seeds, which can make them seem astringent or rough. If a wine's alcohol level is high (over 13.5 percent), it could feel "hot" going down, like a shot of vodka or brandy. None of these descriptions are "either-or" – they're all points on a continuum. Only your personal taste determines where liking ends and disliking begins.

Next, ask yourself how the wine *tastes*. In young wines, the predominant tastes are fruity, perhaps combined with the toast and vanilla flavors sometimes evident in oak-aged red wines and chardonnay.

After several years in the bottle, some wines become more harmonious and subtle, and the individual flavors harder to differentiate. The more you pay attention to the specifics of taste and texture – both pleasant and unpleasant – the better you'll remember the wine, and the better you'll be able to describe what you want when you're talking to a wine merchant or waiter.

The experience isn't over when you swallow. You still want to consider the wine's *finish*. A finish can be long, short or non-existent; it can be gentle or harsh; it can bring forth delicious elements of a wine or reveal "off" or unpleasant flavors. Some light, young wines have practically no finish, while some rich, full-bodied wines can be tasted for quite a long time.

Blueprint for a wine tasting

One of the most pleasant ways to practice tasting is to host a wine tasting with friends. If you do it right, the experience should be neither time-consuming nor expensive.

Trained wine tasters can identify faults, which are usually the result of poor winemaking. Among typical faults are "off" aromas like vinegar, burnt matches, damp cardboard or rotten eggs; inappropriate colors (for example, a young dry white wine that's a brownish color, or a red wine that's strangely light in color); cloudiness; foreign matter or other weird stuff floating around in the wine. Due to advances in winemaking technology, such faults are increasingly rare, but they do occur. A bad cork or exposure to heat during shipping can also ruin wine, making it taste musty or oxidized, like sherry.

Sometimes a fault is so obvious that just about anyone will notice it. At other times, a fault is present in such a small degree that only a trained taster can detect it. Some tasters are particularly sensitive to the odor of sulfur, for example, while others can smell it only when it is quite strong. If a wine looks, smells or tastes odd, take it back to the retailer, who should not object to replacing it - he will just return it to the distributor, who will return it to the winery.

The most important element is the guests. Choose them carefully. When I plan tastings, I make a point of avoiding self-proclaimed wine experts who get a kick out of showing how much they know. (It's almost always less than they think, by the way.) Wine columnist Dave McIntyre summed these folks up as people who "mistakenly believe a wine can only be improved by the sound of their own voices." Instead, I invite friends who enjoy discovering new wines and listening to the opinions of others.

The ideal number of participants is six to ten, depending on how many you can seat at the table. One bottle of each wine will be plenty. A white tablecloth is classic, but many wine buffs just use pieces of ordinary white paper as place mats. Each participant should have some water (paper cups will do). If you like, you can put slices of French baguette on the table. If you don't have enough wine glasses, go to your local restaurant-supply store and buy a case – they're cheap. You can also ask the guests to bring their own glasses, which saves on your cleanup later.

To make sure you can all enjoy the wines' aromas, remind the guests not to wear perfume, cologne or other scented products. Also, sniff the glasses when they're empty to check whether they smell of soap or a musty cupboard. If so, pour a little wine into the glass and carefully turn it so the entire inside is "rinsed." The wine will make most odors disappear.

> When the wines were good they pleased my senses, cheered my spirits, improved my moral and intellectual powers, besides enabling me to confer the same benefits on other people.
> – George Saintsbury,
> *Notes on a Cellar Book*

The biggest difference between professional and hobbyist wine tastings is spitting – pros do it, amateurs don't. (My husband has dubbed my tasting group OPEC, for Organization of People Expectorating Copiously.) Obviously, in normal social situations and at meals, everybody swallows wine. Spitting is appropriate at a tasting when you'll be trying several wines. I have been to meetings of wine appreciation groups where 10 or 12 wines are carefully chosen and obtained by the host, sometimes at great expense. By the time the group arrives at the fifth or sixth wine, everyone is so smashed that they might as well be drinking Boone's Farm. It would certainly be cheaper.

If your goal is to get plastered, then spitting would defeat the purpose. But if you want to taste wines, learn about them and remember them, then it's a waste of time and money *not* to spit. Make spitting easy for people by providing spit cups (one paper coffee cup per person) and dump buckets (one per table of six to eight). It seems yucky at first and people can be shy, but it's the only way to be sure that you learn as much from the last wine as the first.

When it comes to choosing the wines, grape-themed tastings like all-chardonnay or all-cabernet sauvignon are popular. But if your guests aren't yet very familiar with wine, they'll probably find it more meaningful to taste four or five wines that are distinctly different from each other. I'm not much of a fan of the type of tasting where each participant or couple brings a wine, because you can't guarantee that the wines will contrast. Choose a general category, like white wines, red wines or dessert wines, and then ask your wine merchant to help select a variety of wines within the category. Most groups divide the cost of wine among the participants.

A means to an end

One last point about tasting: it is meant to enhance your enjoyment of wine. Too many people get so caught up in the tasting process that they're unable to stop analyzing and comparing. Remember that a wine tasting is a means to an end, a way to sharpen your palate, make new wine discoveries and bring pleasure into your life.

Wine Aroma Wheel

In a scientist's approach to the problem of how to describe wines, Professor Ann C. Noble, Ph.D., a sensory analysis specialist at University of California, Davis, developed the Wine Aroma Wheel. As you can see, the wheel progresses from general aroma descriptions at the outside edge to very specific ones at the center.

The aromas listed on the wheel are just a few of those found in wine, but they offer plenty of options for just about anybody. The precision of these descriptors has really caught on among American wine critics; magazine and newspaper wine reviews are chock full of wine-wheel adjectives. Europeans, by the way, think such lists are absurd, and call these descriptions a fruit salad.

© A.C. Noble 1990
Colored, laminated copies of the Wine Aroma Wheel© can be obtained from A.C. Noble, Department of Viticulture and Enology, University of California, Davis CA 95616. Phone: (530) 752-0387, fax: (530) 752-0382, email: acnoble@ucdavis.edu
All profits go to support wine sensory research.

13

Chapter 3

Is More Than a Grape
A Wine

*In which you consider why most wines are alike,
and how a few are sublimely different*

You're in the supermarket looking for a wine to drink with tonight's dinner. Your thinking process might go something like this: *Hmmm . . . grilled chicken marinated with a little garlic and lemon . . . asparagus . . . there's a sauvignon blanc . . . is that sauvignon blanc we had with chicken at my sister's couple of months ago? . . . it tasted pretty good . . . heck, how wrong can I go for $8.99?* But when you open the wine, it doesn't taste much like the sauvignon blanc you remember. Strange. Weren't both wines made from the same grape?

If you've had a version of that experience, you're not alone. You don't have to pull too many corks before you notice that all wines made from the same grape do not taste alike. Open one cabernet sauvignon and you'll get a mellow, fruity beverage just right for sipping tonight; open another and you'll find a stiff, astringent wine that practically rips the enamel off your teeth. The riesling you bought last week tasted crisp and refreshing; the one you opened yesterday was way too sweet.

Labeling wine by grape variety is a fairly recent development. In Europe, most wines are called by the name of their place of origin. American winemakers, who used Europe as a model for decades, gave many of their wines European names like Chablis, Burgundy or Chianti, even if the wines were nothing like the European originals. American consumers rarely thought about grape variety at all. Eventually, when the wine industry in the United States emerged from the shadow of Europe, high-quality vintners quit borrowing inaccurate foreign names, and American wine drinkers learned to identify wines by grape variety.

Seeing the name of a grape – merlot, sauvignon blanc, riesling – on a label provides much more useful information than a made-up name like blush chablis or Rhine wine. But, as you've seen, one winery's merlot is not necessarily like another's. Lots of people decide to stick with a few tried-and-true wines – but that's not the only way to avoid disappointment. Read on for another approach.

Wine style: the big idea

There are people who look with relish at a shelf full of wines and peruse a wine list as if it were the latest Tom Clancy best seller. They approach wine shopping as an adventure, asking questions of waiters and wine merchants, trying wines from places or producers they've never heard of. How did they get that way? Did it take years of studying wine to feel so confident?

I'll let you in on a secret: You won't get that way overnight, but it's not nearly as hard as it looks. Experienced wine buyers use a few fairly simple strategies to choose wines they like and get good values. All you need to do is consider how wine *tastes* rather than focusing solely on what grape it's made from. In other words, you need to consider *wine style*.

What's a "varietal"?

I hate sounding like a high school English teacher, but I can't help myself. The word varietal is an adjective that the wine industry has turned into a noun. Wines labeled with the names of grapes (such as pinot noir or merlot) are called varietal wines *to distinguish them from wines with geographic labels (such as Chianti or Bordeaux). The phrase was soon shortened to "varietal," as in, "We've got a great selection of varietals on the wine list." Before long, people started calling the grapes themselves "varietals" rather than "varieties." Anyhow, in this book "varietal" is used to describe things, as in "varietal label" or "varietal wine."*

Wine style describes big impressions like fresh, fruity, mellow, lively, smooth, robust, hearty, slightly sweet, rich, full-bodied or tart. If, when you shop, you can describe the style of wine you're looking for, you'll be able to choose among a wider range of wines than if you just named a grape variety. Say "Chardonnay" to a waiter, and she could bring a luscious, golden, oak-aged Santa Barbara wine or a lean, tart Chablis – they're both chardonnay. But order "A rich, full-bodied white wine," and a good wine steward could offer you that Santa Barbara beauty, a New Zealand sauvignon blanc, Rhone Valley white blend or Australian semillon. Your options have just expanded dramatically.

Every wine, from $3 stuff with a screwcap to expensive Bordeaux, has a style, which is the sum of three interrelated factors:

- *The grape*, or blend of grapes
- *The place* where the grapes are grown – the country, the region, sometimes even the vineyard
- *The winemaker*, who shapes the wine.

As you read the rest of this chapter, you'll see that it's impossible to talk about one without the others.

Factor one: grape variety

Grape variety is probably the most influential of the three elements, because it predetermines certain fundamental characteristics of the wine. If the grape is chenin blanc, for example, the wine is going to be white, because chenin blanc is a light-colored grape. The wine will almost surely be light-bodied, because the grape's subtle flavors would get lost under a lot of alcohol and oak. On the other hand, if the grape is zinfandel, the wine will probably be hearty in style and fairly high in alcohol, because zinfandel is usually most flavorful when very ripe, and ripeness translates to high alcohol in a finished wine. You could *try* to make a high-alcohol, oak-aged chenin blanc or a light, delicate zinfandel – and some winemaker probably has – but you'd be fighting each grape's essential nature to do it.

Or compare two red grapes, cabernet sauvignon and pinot noir. Cabernet is a deep purple grape packed with color, flavor and tannin. It naturally makes a robust, deeply colored wine that can be aged for quite a long time in oak barrels without losing its personality. In contrast, pinot noir has fewer pigments than other red grapes, so the wines are generally lighter in color, less tannic and more delicate than cabernet. Its nuanced, elegant nature means that too much aging in oak can be fatal.

Factor two: a sense of place

When it comes to the place the grape is grown, some truths are also self-evident. Geography, geology, climate and similar aspects of planet Earth are pretty much fixed, at least in the short term. I can say with total confidence that the Germans, whose vineyards are Europe's northernmost, are not going to be planting Mediterranean grape varieties like grenache or syrah any time soon (at least not until global warming gets completely out of control). If certain vineyards in Burgundy have been producing heavenly pinot noir for a century, no one in his right mind is going to rip them out and replant with sauvignon blanc. No matter how skillful a winemaker may be, chardonnay grapes zapped to ripeness in the sizzling sun of California's San Joaquin Valley (ever driven through Fresno in August?) are not going to make a wine as subtle and nuanced as chardonnay made from grapes that ripen slowly in the warm days and cool nights of Sonoma County's hills.

But *place* in wine also has a far more profound, even mystical, significance. For centuries, a wine and the place it came from were inseparable. Every aspect of winemaking was determined by the climate, weather, topography and traditions of the place. Most grape varieties were grown in just one or two limited regions. Wines were aged in barrels made of wood from a nearby forest. Grapes may have been harvested on a certain saint's day, ripe or not. Maybe the wine remained unbottled, in open vats, until the local priest came to town and gave it his blessing. Dozens of variables added up to a unique taste. Burgundian winemaker Jacques Lardière calls it "the song of the earth."

> *The vineyard and wine are great mysteries. Alone in the vegetable kingdom, the vine gives us a true understanding of the savor of the earth. And how faithfully it is translated! Through it we realize that even flint can be living, yielding, nourishing. Even the unemotional chalk weeps in wine, golden tears.*
> – Colette, *Prisons et Paradis*

Today, that uniqueness has all but disappeared. Most wines are now made in a style known as *fruit-forward* or *fruit-driven*, which focuses on grape variety and largely ignores the wine's origin. The "Big Three" grape varieties, chardonnay, merlot and cabernet sauvignon, are grown virtually everywhere, from France, Italy and Spain to Bulgaria, California, Oregon, Washington, New York, Hungary, Australia, New Zealand, Chile, Argentina and South Africa. Barrels made of French oak, imparting the same flavors to every wine, are shipped to wineries from Tasmania to Lebanon to Walla Walla, Washington. Regional differences in winemaking techniques are all but gone. American winemakers apprentice in France, Australians work in Oregon, New Zealanders supervise harvests in northern Italy, and everybody reads the same scientific journals and hires the same globe-trotting consultants.

You might wonder what I'm griping about. Modern technology has assured that there's more consistently good-tasting wine available today at reasonable prices than at any other time in history. A well-made bottle of wine, wherever it comes from, tastes just fine in many situations. But something is missing. A big part of wine's magic is the way a liquid in a bottle can embody the soul of a place.

"Somewhere" is different from "anywhere"

Even today, a few wines have a "somewhereness" that makes them recognizable as the product of a region, a district, a vintage and sometimes even a specific vineyard. When you taste a wine with a sense of place, you won't just say, "Nice chardonnay." You'll be able to say, "That flinty aroma, it's got to be Chablis." You won't just say, "Nice shiraz." You'll think of hot, dusty Australia and say, "There's the leathery smell of Hunter Valley shiraz." You won't just say, "Nice sangiovese." Instead, for a split second, you'll be standing on a hill in Chianti, watching sunlight glint off the rooftops of Siena.

Wines that can produce that effect – some prestigious and pricey, some inexpensive treasures – have complex aromas described with words like earthy, herbal, mushroomy or flowery rather than simply fruity. If they're aged in oak, the oak flavors will be integrated into the total taste, rather than standing out as pure vanilla or sweet spice the way they do in many bottlings. They're harder to describe, but they evoke so much more. When it's time to separate the good wines from the great wines, it's somewhereness that makes the difference.

The French name for this elusive, impossible-to-define evocation of a place is *terroir* (*tare-WAHR*). The word is derived from *terra*, Latin for "earth," which makes it sound as if it refers to soil type. But you can't explain the differences among wines simply by whether the grapes are grown on clay soil, slate or gravel. Terroir encompasses all the factors that make a place unique, including soil and subsoil chemistry, climate, vineyard exposure, vintage, topography, elevation, and the relationship of the vineyard to lakes, rivers or the sea. Other variables may include how vineyards are planted, pruned and cultivated. A region's traditional winemaking practices may also contribute to the distinctive quality of certain wines.

Winemakers who seek to express terroir in their wines haven't

You're taking a snapshot of Mother Nature when you crush grapes and make wine. Nothing else can do it with more accuracy than a well-made bottle of wine from a carefully tended vineyard.

– Michael J. Caldwell, *Varietal Tendencies*

rejected modern technology. However, they've made a commitment to identifying the unique synergy between a grape and a place, and to using technology that retains the special taste rather than processing and filtering it away. They're taking a risk that at least some wine buyers will enjoy the unaccustomed tastes that come from being faithful to the character of the land.

Many winemakers call the whole idea of terroir a kind of voodoo designed mainly to keep prices high on certain European wines from well-known regions and vineyards. They say that eventually scientists will analyze all aspects of

"A memorable wine is as much a map as a taste," says Mario Schwenn, owner of Dievole, an estate in Chianti Classico. At Italy's biggest wine trade show, Schwenn demonstrated his devotion to terroir by trucking in a load of soil from Dievole and dumping it on the floor of his display.

these allegedly unique spots and figure out how to replicate the wines elsewhere. It hasn't happened yet. Great wine defies being reduced to a formula. The puzzle of terroir is not about to be solved any time soon.

Factor three: the hand of the winemaker

The third element, the winemaker, puts it all together. She takes the first two elements – grape variety and place of origin – and transforms them into wine. (For simplicity's sake, I'm using "winemaker" as shorthand for the team of vineyardists and winemakers who work together throughout the process.) She makes dozens of decisions every step of the way, from how the grapes are grown through the final release of the bottled wine into the marketplace. When to prune the vines and how much, when to harvest, what methods to use to crush the grapes, what fermentation temperature to use, when fermentation is over, whether to age the wine in barrels and for how long, whether to filter before bottling: these are just a few of the winemaker's concerns.

Good winemakers insist that they're just getting out of the way and letting the wine make itself. Certainly, without ripe, flavorful grapes grown in an appropriate spot, even the Michaelangelo of winemakers wouldn't have a prayer of making a good wine. Yet winemakers still make crucial choices about the best way to bring a wine to life, even if those choices are simply to watch carefully, interfere very little, and avoid processes they consider intrusive or artificial. The winemaker's decisions, big and small, determine the taste of the wine you open at your dinner table.

Where in the world...?

The following location-related terms are frequently part of discussions about wine.

Old World/New World: Old World *means Europe and the Mediterranean.* New World *refers to places that were colonized by Europeans. In general, Old World wines have earthier flavors than New World wines, and are called by the name of the place they're grown rather than by grape variety. New World wines are chiefly identified by grape variety, though a region is included on labels.*

Northern Hemisphere/Southern Hemisphere: *Europe, the Mediterranean and North America are the most important wine regions of the Northern Hemisphere. Major wine-growing areas of the Southern Hemisphere include South Africa, South America (primarily Chile and Argentina), Australia and New Zealand.*

Warm-climate growing areas/Cool-climate growing areas: *If you look at a globe, you can see the two temperate bands where most wine grapes are grown. They are located, roughly, between 30 and 50 degrees both north and south of the equator. In the Northern Hemisphere, wine grapes are grown in the Old World from North Africa to southern England and in the New World from Southern California to British Columbia. In the Southern Hemisphere, the southernmost wine-growing areas are Tasmania (the extreme south of Australia) and the Central Otago region of New Zealand, and the northernmost are in South America, in the southern regions of Peru and Bolivia.*

This concept is important because Mediterranean grape varieties like grenache, syrah and malbec grow best in warm climates, while Continental varieties like riesling and pinot noir thrive in cool climates. In general, the closer to the equator, the warmer the growing region, though conditions vary based on maritime influence, altitude of the vineyards, location of valleys and mountain ranges and other factors.

Chapter 4

Wine Geography Made Easy

*In which you tour nations and appellations,
and learn how to scrutinize labels*

*E*ven if you're one of those people who never asks for directions
no matter how lost you get, you'll want to learn to navigate through
the terrain of wine. Being familiar with the basics of wine geography,
and especially how it relates to quality, is an essential step on the way
to being a confident, well-informed wine consumer.

This chapter tells how hemispheres, borders, regions and even
smaller divisions of the map create a hierarchy of wine value. It also
explains how the information on wine labels can help you find a
good-tasting, good-value bottle for your dinner table. You don't need
to memorize a bunch of French or Italian place names or study a map
of Mendocino County to understand the underlying principles, which
are the same for any place in the wine-growing world.

> *As in a great
> magic act, you
> shouldn't be able
> to see the hand of
> the winemaker.
> Only the voice of
> the vineyard
> should be heard.*
> – Lalou
> Bize-Leroy

Appellations explained

A designated geographic area where wine is produced is called
an *appellation* (pronounced in English like the *Appalachian* mountains).
Like so many terms that now apply to all wines, it originated in
France. The French *appellation d'origine controlée* is the world's most
complex and complete system for regulating wine quality. *Appellation*
means "name" or "designation": *d'origine controlée* means "of controlled
(verified) origin." The phrase is sometimes abbreviated AC.

Appellations were developed in France during the 1930s, an era
when fraud and adulteration of wine were widespread. Wines were
"stretched" with water or "strengthened" with sugar before fermentation.
Robust, cheap wine from southern France and North Africa was used
to "improve" the color and flavor of wines from cooler regions such as
Burgundy. Once the fraud became known, serious wine lovers

demanded some assurance that they were getting the wine they'd paid for. Ethical producers needed a way to certify that their wines were the real thing. Everyone wanted some kind of credible quality control.

From the very beginning, then, a French appellation signified more than a place on a map. Every appellation has regulations on such things as grape varieties, grape ripeness at harvest, minimum and maximum alcoholic strength of the finished wines, vineyard yields and other viticultural practices, and many technical aspects of the winemaking process. Government inspectors enforce the rules.

American appellations

In the United States, an appellation of origin can be the name of a country, a state or states (if grapes come from two states), or a county or counties within a state. We've also got more than 100 *American Viticultural Areas* (AVAs), part of a French-inspired system that was adopted by the federal government in 1978. All AVAs are appellations of origin, but only some appellations of origin are AVAs. In Oregon, for example, Yamhill County is within the Willamette Valley AVA, so on some wines, you'll see the appellation "Yamhill County" and on others you'll see "Willamette Valley." Both are legal; the decision is up to the winery.

AVA boundaries don't necessarily follow state or county lines. Instead, they designate wine growing areas which are supposed to be distinctive in some way. When wineries in a given area want an AVA, they get together and petition for approval from the Bureau of Alcohol, Tobacco and Firearms (ATF), which oversees wine labeling. If approved, the name can be used on labels.

The important thing to remember is that AVAs are not designations of quality. According to ATF regulations, AVAs were established to "help consumers better identify the wines they may purchase, and help winemakers distinguish their products from wines made in other

> ### What's up, DOC?
>
> *In 1963, emulating the French, the Italians began a system called* denominazione d'origine controllata (DOC), *which included many features of the French ACs, at least on paper. However, if the purpose of an appellation system is to identify wines of quality for the consumer, then the fact that more than 700 wines have DOC standing confuses the issue, to say the least.*
>
> *A higher designation,* DOCG (denominazione d'origine controllata e garantita – *controlled and guaranteed), has been granted to only 11 consistently excellent wines.*

areas." In other words, they're marketing tools for wineries. Some appellations, like Napa Valley, Carneros, Rutherford, Oakville or Stag's Leap, have developed reputations for quality. The vast majority, however, mean little to most consumers.

Hitting the bull's-eye

Picture a target made up of concentric circles getting progressively smaller to the bull's-eye in the center. In an archery competition, the closer an arrow comes to the center, the higher the score. A bull's-eye, which is rare, is worth the most points.

10 — *Country*
20 — *Region*
30 — *Region*
40 — *Region*
50 — *Vineyard*

Wine geography works the same way: there are appellations within appellations within appellations, and the "score" gets higher as the target gets smaller. The smaller a wine's appellation, the more it reflects the unique qualities of its terroir, and the rarer (and more expensive) it will probably be.

Take a bottle of New World chardonnay, for example. The outermost ring of the target can represent a country, the United States. Within that ring is a smaller ring representing a state, California. You can easily buy a chardonnay labeled "California" for $10.

10 — *United States*
20 — *California*
30 — *Sonoma County*
40 — *Russian River Valley*
50 — *Dutton Ranch Vineyard*

Within California (and inside the California ring) is Sonoma County. Continue moving toward the center of the target to the next ring, Russian River Valley, and then to the bull's-eye, Dutton Ranch Vineyard. With each move, the aromas and flavors of the wines should have more distinctive characteristics. Dutton Ranch Vineyard is the source of a top chardonnay from Kistler Vineyards, an outstanding producer. A bottle of Kistler Dutton Ranch Chardonnay will cost at least $50, though you'd be lucky to find any at all.

This system originated in France, where you'll find more rings in the target and a wider range of quality and price than almost anywhere else. Consider a bottle of French pinot noir. The outermost ring is the country, and the next is the region of Burgundy (*Bourgogne* in French). The next step toward the bull's-eye is the Côte de Nuits, a small region renowned for red wines, then the village of Vosne-Romanée. Finally you reach La Tache, one of the world's greatest vineyards for pinot noir. A wine simply labeled "Bourgogne" might cost $10 to $12; for a bottle of La Tache from Domaine de la Romanée-Conti, figure $800 to $1000, depending on the vintage.

A wine label will not necessarily show *every* ring of the target, but it will almost always show the country of origin and usually the smallest applicable designation, because that's the one that matters most. The chart below shows a few examples of New World and Old World geographical designations, organized from country to vineyard, left to right. Good wines can come from any level; in some regions there might be fewer levels, or vineyard names might not be used at all. As you move toward the right and the "score" gets higher, you're more likely to find truly unique wines.

(There's more about labels in the next section, and a *lot* more about French labels in Chapter 11, Cruisin' Through the Crus.)

10 points *Country*	20 points *Region*	30 points *Region*	40 points *Region*	50 points *Vineyard*
New World				
United States	California	Santa Barbara County	Santa Ynez Valley	Sanford & Benedict
United States	Washington	Columbia Valley	Walla Walla Valley	Canoe Ridge
Australia	South Australia	Barossa Valley	—	Pewsey Vale
New Zealand	—	Marlborough	Awatere Valley	Vavasour
Old World				
France	Bourgogne	Cote de Nuits	Nuits-St.-Georges	Les Cailles
France	Bourgogne	Cote de Beaune	Meursault	Les Santenots
France	Chablis	Chablis Grand Cru	—	Vaudésir
France	Bordeaux	Médoc	Margaux	Chateau Palmer
Italy	Valpolicella	Valpolicella Classico	—	Palazzo alla Torre

Labels and fables

The information on labels falls into three categories:
- both required and regulated by law
- not required by law but still regulated
- unregulated marketing gobbledygook.

Whether wines are made in the United States or imported from abroad, the labels used here must be approved by the Bureau of Alcohol, Tobacco and Firearms (ATF), a division of the Treasury Department.

Wine labels, like the labels on other food packages, are meant to give you a technically accurate picture of the contents. A label can't answer the most important question – will you like what's inside? – but it sure can help you narrow down your choices and take your best shot. Here are some typical wine-shopping questions and the answers you can get from a label.

When wine importer Kermit Lynch wanted to put a quotation from Thomas Jefferson on his labels, he found himself in the kafkaesque position of convincing a federal agency that the words of a Founding Father could be distributed to the American public. Lynch finally won ATF approval, and now every bottle from Kermit Lynch Imports carries Jefferson's revolutionary sentiment, "Good wine is a necessity of life for me."

Who made the wine?

The name of a winery is almost always on the label. This sounds obvious, but it's very important, because the most reliable way to buy wine is to identify consistent producers and seek out their wines.

Which grapes are in the bottle?

If a grape variety (merlot or sauvignon blanc, for example) is named on the label, then the wine must contain a minimum of 75 percent of that grape. For most wines made in Oregon and Washington, the requirement is higher, 90 percent. This is your guarantee that when you buy something labeled merlot, you're getting (mostly) merlot.

Until 1983, federal law set the minimum required amount of the named grape variety at only 51 percent. The law changed because American consumers were buying increasing amounts of varietal wines and they demanded a truthfully labeled product. The law also helped level the playing field among wineries, so that quality-oriented producers who made legitimate varietal wines wouldn't be beaten out in the marketplace by producers using a bare minimum of expensive grapes.

If more than one grape variety is used, and no single variety makes up 75 percent of the wine, the label can list more than one grape in order of prominence in the wine. Common examples are Semillon Chardonnay and Cabernet Merlot.

How old is the wine?

If there's a vintage date on the label, then at least 95 percent of the wine must come from that vintage.

Where were the grapes grown?

Federal law says the name of a state can appear on a label if at least 75 percent of the grapes were grown in that state. If grapes were grown in two states and neither state was the origin of 75 percent of the blend, then "American" is used instead. However, some states have stricter rules. If you want to use "California" on your label, for example, California law requires that 100 percent of the grapes be grown in the Golden State.

What did the winery actually do, anyway?

A plethora of confusing government-approved terms indicate all sorts of stuff, like whether the winery owns the vineyard, leases the vineyard or simply buys the grapes; whether the winery itself is located in the same appellation as the one in which the grapes are grown; and whether the winery crushes the grapes or has them crushed elsewhere, to name just a few possibilities.

Perfectly good wines can be made with grapes acquired in many different ways. To me, the reputation of the producer and the quality of the finished wine are much more important than exactly where the grapes were crushed or grown. Of all the possible terms, I find two meaningful: *estate bottled* or *grown, produced and bottled by Winery X*. Both indicate that a winery has tended the grapes from vineyard to bottle. They signify a winery's commitment to producing distinctive wines by controlling the process from beginning to end.

Creative label terminology

The law leaves a lot of leeway for subjective description. It's okay to say a red wine smells like "black cherries, pepper and spice," even if the aromas exist mostly in the winemaker's imagination and the label has neglected to mention a big whiff of rubber. Meaningless phrases

Wine is under suspicion, as beautiful things often are. Like religion, love, laughter, any sort of explosive, it is an anxiety to officials.
- Christopher Morley,
The Romany Stain

like "handcrafted," "uncompromising quality, distinctive style and undeniable appeal" or "a generous palate that finishes rich and firm," are common and perfectly permissible, though utterly useless. So are hopelessly general food recommendations, like "Drink with pasta, chicken and seafood."

A few terms to view with skepticism:

Reserve originally meant wine that was superior in some way to the winery's other bottlings, so it was set aside (reserved) and bottled separately. Reserve wines may be aged longer than regular bottlings, or subjected to some other special winemaking technique. The term implies higher quality and almost always guarantees a higher price tag.

In reality, a winery can define *reserve* any way it wants to. Sometimes you'll see the term used on low-end wines in an attempt to add cachet. In Europe the use of the term is largely controlled by law, requiring a certain amount of aging in oak barrels, for example.

Cuvée (*cue-VAY*) is a classy-sounding word that comes from a French term for "vat" or "tank." In the United States, it has acquired a meaning similar to *reserve*, suggesting a batch or container of wine that has been set aside for some special reason, presumably because of its quality. You may have seen American wines labeled *special cuvée* or, for the French touch, *cuvée speciale*. Since the term is not regulated by law, it can be used on any wine, special or not.

Old vines raises the question, "How old is old?" Most grape vines don't bear a significant crop until at least three years after they have been planted, and are still considered very young for a decade or so. When young, vines produce so prolifically that the grape grower's biggest problem is usually limiting the crop, because large harvests mean diluted, one-dimensional flavors. In France, certain appellations even prohibit wines made from very young vines from carrying the appellation name. Such wines are placed in a lower quality classification, *vin de pays*, until the vines attain a certain age.

Vines can live for decades, and over time they produce smaller and smaller crops. Just as an abundant crop usually results in diluted flavors, a small crop from older vines produces grapes with more intense and complex flavors. Wine critics and knowledgeable consumers are aware of the advantages of older vineyards, and old vines – in French, *vieilles vignes (vee-AY VEEN-yuh)* – on a label carries a promise of a more flavorful, more distinctive wine.

Problem is, there's no legal definition an old vine, either here or in Europe. The decision to put the term on a label is entirely up to the winery, with no guidelines at all from the authorities about what it means. (However, if the label *specifically* states that all the grapes came from an 80-year-old vineyard, say, then that information must be true, because U.S. law requires labels to be truthful.)

The French classification vin de pays (van duh pay–EE, *meaning "country wine") is one notch down from an* appellation controllée *but is still meant to signify a wine with regional character and identity. VdPs often represent fine value for the money. When you see a French wine with a varietal label like Chardonnay or Syrah, it's usually a VdP, and chances are that it's labeled* Vin de Pays d'Oc (van duh pay–EE DOCK), *which means it's from the Languedoc in southern France, the country's biggest source of varietal wines.*

Barrel-aged and/or barrel-fermented are phrases frequently used on labels. When you see these terms, some of the wine certainly saw the inside of a barrel, but how much or for how long is anybody's guess. If you smell oaky aromas like vanilla or toast, they could have been produced by dunking a giant teabag of oak chips into wine in a stainless steel tank, one of several ways to avoid expensive, time-consuming barrel aging. Even experienced tasters can't always tell how a wine acquired its oak aromas.

I'm not saying that wineries are trying to deceive consumers. Most of them aren't. But especially at the lower end of the price scale, take the prose and promises on the labels with a grain of salt.

Chapter 5

Meet the Grapes

*In which each grape reveals
its own personality, and you read of
muscat and musk, but no muskrats*

 = Red Wine

 = White Wine

By now, you've probably got the idea that you won't attain wine nirvana by considering grape variety alone. Still, knowing your grape varieties is an essential part of the map to finding your way through the world of wine. Every wine begins with a grape, and grape variety is the least flexible and most influential of the three factors (grape, place and winemaker) that determine the taste of a wine. It's not the *only* thing to know, but it's an *important* thing.

Here's an opinionated guide to the most popular grape varieties – how they taste, how and where they're made, and why you should consider drinking them.

 ## Cabernet sauvignon
Bordeaux

Cabernet sauvignon, nicknamed "cab" by enthusiasts, is the heaviest of wine's heavy hitters, the Mark McGwire of grapes. It's the major grape in the wines of Bordeaux. It's the grape that put California on the wine world's map. It's eminently age-worthy. Critics rave about it and well-heeled collectors around the world pay a bundle for wines from the top French châteaus and California boutique wineries. No question about it, cab's got cachet.

Most of us aren't buying cab at $3000 a case and burying it in the cellar for 20 years. Still, the grape must have some appeal at the real-people end of the price scale or it couldn't be as popular as it is.

Good cabernet, at any price, should have substantial fruit – the classic description is black currant, and berry and plum aromas are typical. Cab often has herbaceous aromas like mint or eucalyptus; when the grapes aren't quite ripe, however, the wine can develop unpleasant asparagus or bell pepper scents. Earthy or dusty scents

A varietal label identifies wine by grape variety rather than geographic origin. A varietal wine has a varietal label.

The plural of château can be spelled two ways – châteaus and châteaux – but all three words are pronounced the same way: sha-TOE.

aren't uncommon in fine cabs. Almost all cabernet spends a goodly period aging in oak barrels (usually French oak), which add complementary aromas like vanilla, smoke, clove and cedar.

The big drawback to enjoying cabernet is tannin. Tannin in wine is a good news/bad news deal: you need tannin if you want a red wine to age well, yet too much of it makes young wines astringent and bitter. To make the deeply colored, intensely flavored style of cabernet that collectors demand, the juice must spend quite a long time in contact with the skins, which are also the main source of tannin. In the quest to make ever more impressive and long-lived wines, many New World winemakers have become famous (some would say notorious) for not sparing the tannin. New oak barrels, which are lavishly used for aging cabernet, also impart tannin, of a harsher-tasting type than the tannin found in grape skins.

Cabernet sauvignon is a tough, thick-skinned grape that grows well and ripens easily in a number of different conditions. Because of its popularity, its ability to add depth and power to other varieties, and its obliging way of growing under many different conditions, you can find cabernet in most of the world's wine regions. In France, besides Bordeaux, cab is planted in the vast Languedoc region; in Tuscany it is blended with sangiovese, and in Spain it's a partner for tempranillo.

The Napa Valley is Ground Zero for cabernet in the United States. Highly touted bottlings are also come from other regions of California and from the Yakima Valley, Columbia Valley and Walla

What are Bordeaux blends?

More and more, New World winemakers are realizing what the vintners of Bordeaux have long known: cabernet tastes best when blended with complementary grape varieties that tone down its harsher qualities. Bordeaux are usually blends of cabernet and merlot, and many contain small amounts of cabernet franc or other grapes. Blends of these grapes are being made just about anywhere that cabernet and merlot are both grown.

A lot of California cabernets have been blended with a little merlot for years, but as long as the wines contain at least 75 percent cabernet, they can legally carry the varietal label Cabernet Sauvignon. However, when Californians started making Bordeaux-style blends that contained less than 75 percent of any one variety, they couldn't use a single grape variety on the label. A new name, Meritage (rhymes with heritage), was invented to describe Bordeaux blends from California.

Walla appellations of Washington. The Australians, who have the climate and soils for terrific red wines, grow cabernet in many areas, notably Coonawarra. For good value, look to Chile and Argentina.

If you like the flavors of cab but want to drink it young, look for buzzwords like "smooth" or "accessible" on the labels (or buy merlot instead). Generally, the lighter-bodied cabs are least expensive.

Chardonnay
Burgundy, Chablis

Americans are in love with chardonnay. The name has become so familiar that some people think it's a synonym for white wine. And in one way, it is: chardonnay is the largest selling varietal wine in the United States. A possible explanation for chardonnay's popularity – besides how easy it is to pronounce the name – is that it is often less acidic than other white wines and has the sweet aromas of oak aging.

Chardonnay's traditional home is Burgundy, where it's made into some of the world's greatest and highest priced white wines. A great white Burgundy is a silky wine, with complex aromas of fruit and earth, a core of acidity and a buttery richness in the mouth. White Burgundy is frequently aged in oak.

Chardonnay is also the grape of Chablis, in the northernmost part of Burgundy, where it tends to make wine that's crisper and more acidic, with delicate fruit and mineral aromas. Some producers age Chablis in oak, and some do not.

When Americans think of chardonnay, they usually envision the Napa Valley style: rich, with soft acidity, buttery flavors, high alcohol (often 14 percent or more), a creamy texture and the scrumptious aromas that come from new French oak, such as vanilla, smoke, toast, clove and cinnamon. This style has millions of defenders and a few cranky detractors, who admire the leaner wines of Chablis.

Almost anything you'll read about matching wine and food will say that heavy oak aromas, low acidity and high alcohol are not particularly compatible with food. None of this advice has ever swayed chardonnay-lovers from enjoying the wine on all occasions, nor should it.

After reviewing 30 years of research on the health benefits of wine, French cardiologist Jean-Paul Broustet concluded that cabernet sauvignon, especially from Bordeaux, is the healthiest of all wines. Cabernet contains the highest concentrations of resveratrol and quercitin, compounds that promote cardiovascular health. Dr. Broustet lives in Bordeaux, of course.

Chenin Blanc
Loire Valley, Savennières, Vouvray, Coteaux du Layon

Just about all white wines are under-appreciated today, but chenin blanc is even more unappreciated than most. Part of the problem is that most Americans last saw "chenin blanc" on the label of a jug wine being poured into plastic cups in their college dorm rooms.

In the Loire Valley, however, chenin blanc makes absolutely world-class wines, ranging from delicate, bone-dry bottlings to satiny, honeyed sweet wines. Fine chenin blancs are fragrant with the aromas of pears, melons, peaches and apricots, and often have mineral aromas typical of the areas in which they're grown. Like most French wines, these are not labeled by grape variety but by region, such as Savennières (dry), Vouvray (dry to sweet styles), and Coteaux du Layon (where the dessert wines are to die for, especially the ones from the subregion called Quarts de Chaume).

For food-friendliness, chenin blanc is right up there with riesling, yet it's so out of fashion that prices are ridiculously low, even for the best wines.

 Gamay Noir
Beaujolais

Gamay noir, also known simply as gamay, is the grape of Beaujolais, the southernmost part of Burgundy. Wines labeled simply Beaujolais (*BO-jo-LAY*) are generally light-bodied, with berry and cherry flavors, a minimum of tannin and a moderate alcohol level. On shelves in the United States, you're likely to see wines from Beaujolais Villages, a more limited appellation within the larger region, where the wines are fuller-bodied than simple Beaujolais and generally have more character and more intense fruit aromas.

The highest quality Beaujolais comes from 10 specific villages, known collectively as the *cru Beaujolais*. The wines vary in weight and style according to the producer; the best are sturdy, medium-bodied wines with deep plummy and earthy flavors. Beaujolais Villages rarely costs much more than $10; cru Beaujolais can cost up to $20.

Every year about the third week in November, the wine world goes nuts over *Beaujolais nouveau* (*BO-jo-LAY new-VO*), a "new" wine that tastes like grape juice, stains your teeth blue and should be drunk immediately, if not sooner. In most wine growing regions, these slightly fizzy new wines are guzzled at harvest festivals and forgotten before the hangovers disappear.

Savennières spreads across the palate like cream, revealing glimpses of flavor like an ever-changing landscape.

— Jacqueline Friedrich,
A Wine and Food Guide to the Loire

Relentless marketing of Beaujolais nouveau has turned it from an ancient harvest-time tradition into an international phenomenon, airlifted to enthusiasts from Tokyo to Manhattan who await the wine's arrival like members of a cargo cult scanning the horizon for the Messiah.

Drinking Beaujolais nouveau can be a lot of fun if you're surrounded by fellow revelers, but so can chugging green beer on St. Patrick's Day. For myself, I can think of dozens of wines I'd rather drink for the $10-or-so I'd pay for nouveau.

In the United States, only a tiny amount of gamay noir is grown. The grapes called gamay beaujolais and Napa gamay, both grown in California, are distinct from gamay noir, and used mostly in jug wines.

Gewurztraminer

Despite its Teutonic-sounding name, relatively little gewurztraminer (*guh-VURTZ-tra-meen-er*, but wine pros just say *ge-VURTZ*) is grown in Germany. The world's benchmark gewurz – bone dry, flinty and bursting with intriguing aromas of peaches, roses, grapefruit, honey and nutmeg – comes from Alsace, in northeast France. The skin of the gewurztraminer grape is a pinkish-golden color, so the wines are often darker in color than other dry whites, with a rosy glow.

Gewurz translates into English as "spicy," but, frankly, the wine has never seemed particularly spicy to me. Intriguing, yes, intense, aromatic and surprising, but not spicy. The spicy connection must be why gewurz is often recommended as a partner for spicy foods, especially Asian cuisines. The wine has food-friendly acidity and fruitiness, to be sure, but it's often high in alcohol – a no-no with spicy foods. The combo can work, but it's always seemed counter-productive to me to put a wine with such complex flavors together with such complex foods.

With simple nibbles like toasted nuts, smoked trout and creamy cheeses, gewurztraminer makes a top-notch aperitif, because there's so much interesting stuff going on in the glass. I also enjoy it with fairly unadorned foods, like roast chicken or pork tenderloin with a simple marinade of soy sauce and orange.

Finding a good dry American gewurztraminer isn't easy. Most are somewhat sweet and simple-minded, but dry, complex versions do exist. For true gewurztraminer nuts, Alsace is definitely the hot ticket. The Alsatians also make swoon-inducing gewurztraminer dessert wines, redolent of rose petals, pineapple and mango.

Those who like this sort of thing will find that this is the sort of thing they like.
– Max Beerbohm

Grenache
Côtes-du-Rhône, Châteauneuf-du-Pape, Gigondas, Vacqueyras

Grenache (*gren-NAHSH*) is most often made in an easy-drinking, light-bodied style, smelling of strawberries or cherries. At a meal it's rarely the main attraction. It's more likely to play second fiddle to vibrant foods like barbecued ribs, grilled fish or tomato-topped pizza. Grenache is often blended with other grapes, especially in delicious grenache-shiraz blends from Australia. Inexpensive grenache should be drunk within a couple of years of the vintage date.

In the southern Rhône Valley, grenache is a workhorse grape. Wines from the Côtes-du-Rhône, an appellation that encompasses almost 100,000 acres of vineyard, are the least expensive and distinctive examples. Many think of Côtes-du-Rhône as a generic red wine, although a quality producer can turn out something both drinkable and affordable. Côtes-du-Rhône Villages wines are somewhat higher in alcohol and fuller-bodied. If you should come across a Vacqueyras or Gigondas, try it and you'll see how well grenache works as an earthier, more rustic wine.

Grenache makes its bid for immortality in Châteauneuf-du-Pape, an appellation in the southern Rhône just across the river from the city of Avignon. It is the major grape among the 13 varieties legally permitted in Châteauneuf-du-Pape, where the wines are big, bold and age-worthy.

Malbec
Cahors

Red wine lovers, take note: malbec is on the way. Big, lush, fruity and often tannic, it's a good-value, casual, unpolished red. Though planted in several parts of France (notably Cahors, where the grape is called *cot*), malbec turns up as a varietal wine most often from Chile and Argentina, and is often blended with cabernet or merlot.

Châteauneuf-du-Pape means "the pope's new castle." The story goes that in 1309, Pope Clement V left Rome for Avignon because of political intrigue at the Vatican. The guys at the Vatican said, "Nyah, nyah, spoilsport" (roughly translated) and elected a different pope, who ruled in Rome. Everybody had kissed and made up by 1377, when Pope Gregory XI took the papal court back to Rome.

Merlot
Bordeaux

Merlot, frequently blended with cabernet sauvignon in Bordeaux, is the best-selling red wine in the United States. It offers a lot of the good stuff that cabernet has – fruit, color, boldness, big sensations – but in a lusher, friendlier way, and without so much of that nasty tannin. Wine producers the world over have gambled big time that the merlot phenomenon will continue, by planting huge acreages of the variety.

 Muscat
Asti-Spumante, Moscato d'Asti

There are dozens of varieties of muscat – orange muscat, black muscat, muscat ottonel, muscat of Alexandria and *muscat blanc à petits grains*, to name just a few – which are found all over the wine-growing world, and known for their intense perfumes. (See the connection between *muscat* and *musk*?) The aromas make the grape ideal for sweet wines, which complement citrus, ginger and nut desserts. Occasionally you'll encounter a dry muscat, most likely from Alsace.

Asti-Spumante (*AHS-tee spoo-MAHN-tay*) and Moscato d'Asti (*mo-SKAH-toe DAHS-tee*), two charming off-dry bubblies from northern Italy, are made from muscat as well. These wines, which are often as low as five percent alcohol, taste terrific with flavors often found in wedding cakes, like raspberry, orange, butter, vanilla and almonds. Low alcohol makes them particularly pleasant during hot weather.

 Nebbiolo
Barolo, Barbaresco

Piedmont – the region in the northwestern Italian foothills of the Alps – is home to nebbiolo (*neb-ee-OH-lo*), the grape used to make Barolo (*bar-OH-lo*) and Barbaresco (*bar-bar-ESS-co*), two of Italy's most sought-after wines. Barolo is considered heartier than Barbaresco, but they're both substantial wines that combine big fruit, high acidity and plenty of tannin. The classic description of Barolo is "tar and roses," and it's not for everyone: Italian wine authority Burton Anderson once said, "It takes five years to get used to the taste."

Barolo and Barbaresco are also among Italy's most expensive bottlings, because the wineries are small and most of the wines need aging to be palatable. Some less expensive, lighter-bodied nebbiolo is bottled with the varietal label Nebbiolo delle Langhe.

In 1990, Americans drank 10 million bottles of California merlot. In 1996, the year's total was 62 million. In 1998, according to the California Department of Food and Agriculture, enough merlot was harvested to make 17.3 million cases, or roughly 207.6 million bottles of California merlot.

The word nebbiolo derives from the Italian nebbia, which means "fog" – a logical enough name for a grape grown in the famously foggy Piedmont.

Pinot Blanc/Pinot Bianco

What you've got here are two names for the same grape, the first French, the second Italian. In Alsace, pinot blanc (*PEE-no blahnk*) isn't usually expected to be anything more than a reasonably priced, drinkable, light-bodied wine. Winemakers aim to maximize the grape's delicate fruit flavors and balanced, refreshing acidity. Pinot blanc and pinot blanc blends from Alsace offer good value. A small amount of pinot blanc is also grown in Burgundy.

The winemakers of the Italian Alps have higher expectations for their pinot bianco (*PEE-no bee-AHN-co*). When planted in premium vineyard sites and made with care, Italian pinot bianco can have aromas of ripe peach, lemon and green apple. Both pinot blanc and pinot bianco are versatile, food-friendly wines that mesh with seafood, salads, tomatoes and other hot-weather dishes.

Pinot blanc is grown in both Oregon and California. In Oregon, the wine is generally made with little or no oak aging, using Alsace or Italy as a model. In California, several wineries are making pinot blanc as a chardonnay wannabe, high in alcohol, with soft acidity and a double helping of oaky vanilla and toast.

Pinot Gris/Pinot Grigio

Once again, these are two names for the same grape – pinot gris (*PEE-no gree*) in Alsace and pinot grigio (*PEE-no GREE-gee-o*) in Italy. In Alsace, pinot gris is one of the four grape varieties classified as "noble." (The others, in case you're ever on "Jeopardy!" are riesling, gewurztraminer and muscat.) Pinot gris from Alsace is dry and rich, with a fruity yet not overwhelming aroma. The best pinot gris from Oregon (the only American growing area with significant amounts of the grape) is made in the style of Alsace.

With food, pinot gris is remarkably versatile, and especially delicious with grilled fish and Asian cuisines. In the Pacific Northwest, the richness of pinot gris has made it an ideal match for rich, flavorful grilled Copper River salmon, a wild salmon from Alaska.

Italian pinot grigio ranges from thin, uninteresting, mass-produced wine to crisp, carefully crafted bottlings from the best producers of the Friuli and Trentino-Alto Adige regions (in the Alps, bordering Austria). The best pinot grigio is light and refreshing, with apple, pear and mineral aromas.

Pinot Noir
Bourgogne (Burgundy)

Sum up pinot noir in a few paragraphs? No problem. Just let me finish writing this 25-word summary of *War and Peace*, and I'll get right to it.

Whole books have been written about the red wine of Burgundy. Whole lives have been devoted to making it, collecting it and savoring it. No grape inspires more sighs, squabbles and philosophizing, probably because drinking a truly great Burgundy – subtle, nuanced, powerful, fragrant – is a rare and unforgettable experience.

Very poetic indeed. But if you're more interested in *drinking* wine than contemplating it, you should know that pinot noir (*PEE-no NWAHR*) is the undisputed champion of red wines when it comes to versatility with food. When you're in a restaurant and one person orders salmon, another chooses duck, the third gets lamb and the fourth is a vegetarian who's having a wild mushroom ragout, choosing a wine may look puzzling. It's not. The answer is simple: pinot noir.

Pinot noir is a chameleon. It's just about the only red grape that can be made into convincing light-bodied, medium-bodied and full-bodied wines. With fewer pigments than other red grapes, pinot noir tends to be lighter in color and more subtle in flavor than other red wines. Less tannic than most reds (words like silky or feminine are often used to describe it), it usually has more prominent acidity, increasing its food compatibility.

The pinot noir grape is notorious for giving grape-growers nightmares. It develops the most complex flavors in cooler climates where the possibility of a rainy harvest or a dreary, sun-starved September makes every vintage a gamble. Selection of a vineyard site is crucial, and few vineyards have what it takes to produce outstanding pinot noir. Besides Burgundy, fine pinot noir is made in Oregon's Willamette and Umpqua valleys, California (check labels for cool-weather appellations like Carneros, Russian River and Santa Ynez Valley), New Zealand and some bits of Australia.

You've probably figured out that outstanding pinot noir is rare and can be frightfully expensive. The top labels from Burgundy in a good vintage can cost several hundred dollars a bottle. The best and most complex wines of the New World cost at least $30 and frequently more. However, the soaring popularity of merlot has convinced wine

> *I hope the Burgundy has reached you safely & that you are lapping it with judicious determination.*
> – Winston Churchill in a letter to his wife, Clementine

producers that consumers want affordable red wines that are lighter, less tannic and more versatile than cabernet sauvignon. Look for an increasing number of simple, fruity, drinkable pinot noirs priced at $15 or less, mostly from the New World.

Riesling
Almost all German whites and Alsace

Somebody once asked me, "If you had to choose only one wine to drink for the rest of your life, what would it be?"

A number of possibilities flashed through my mind, but my answer was "riesling." The riesling (*REEZ-ling*) grape is made into wines ranging from light and lively to lush and sweet. It is delicious young, yet ages magnificently. It's grown in many parts of the world, and has a distinct personality in each one. How could I ever be bored? Good chardonnay is like a symphony by Mahler, a lush, deep wall of sound. Riesling is more like a Mozart string quartet. You hear the players together, but you also hear all four parts separately, in perfect balance.

The quality riesling of the Old World comes largely from Germany and the Alsace region of France. In Germany, the world's northernmost wine-growing region, grapes ripen slowly, developing complex flavors and maintaining very high acidity. As a result, most German rieslings are slightly sweet, to balance the acidity that's typical of both the grape and the cool growing region. German riesling can be as low as 8 to 9 percent alcohol compared to other table wines at 12 to 13 percent.

Alsace, too, is located pretty far north, but its weather is moderated by a mountain range, the Vosges, which shelters the region from severe cold. Grapes in Alsace become riper, so the wines are generally richer and higher in alcohol than the German wines. For less than $20 a bottle you can get high quality rieslings from either area which will knock your socks off with flavor and complexity.

Riesling is the ultimate food wine, whether dry or off-dry. Don't let the slight sweetness of some rieslings keep you from trying them with a wide variety of foods. The Germans drink off-dry wines with everything from smoked fish to roast pork, lobster, crab and just about anything with a cream sauces. In Alsace, riesling is the classic accompaniment for *choucroute*, a hearty regional specialty combining pork and sausages on a bed of sauerkraut.

Three tiny but terrific New World regions for dry riesling: New York State's Finger Lakes, Australia's Clare Valley and New Zealand's Martinborough.

Young riesling harmonizes with Chinese, Thai, Vietnamese and Indian foods; older riesling can go well with venison, other game meats and mushroom dishes. The least successful combinations are with the strong flavors of the Mediterranean, like garlic or grilled foods.

 Sangiovese

Chianti, Brunello di Montalcino, Vino Nobile di Montepulciano

Two questions: 1) Have you ever tasted wine made from a grape called *sangiovese* (*san-gee-oh-VAY-say*)? 2) Have you ever tried Chianti, the classic wine of Tuscany?

If you're like most American wine lovers, you answered "no" to the first question and "yes" to the second – proof positive that Chianti (*key-AHN-tee*) may be the best known of all Italian wines, but sangiovese, the grape variety it's made from, has barely made a dent in the collective wine-drinking consciousness.

Chianti is made in a wide range of styles, from fairly light, fruity, slightly earthy wines to more robust *riserva* wines that have been aged in oak for three years before bottling. The large Chianti region, covering most of Tuscany, encompasses a number of subregions, including the well-known Chianti Classico. (Authentic Chianti Classico wines have a black rooster – *gallo nero* in Italian – on the neck labels.)

Looking at what the Tuscans themselves eat provides some good ideas for food matches. Their signature dish is grilled steak (*bistecca alla fiorentina*) and they traditionally eat braised meats, flavorful game like hare and wild boar, sausages and meat-sauced and tomato-sauced pastas. Stay away from foods with sweet sauces, which will make these high-acid wines taste sour.

During the 1990s, a number of California winemakers started growing sangiovese for varietal wines, which has made the grape name somewhat more familiar. And in Italy, a new quality designation called IGT – *indicazione geografica tipica*, similar to the French *vin de pays* – brought sangiovese with varietal labels to the U.S. marketplace at very reasonable prices. One rung below Chianti on the quality ladder, IGTs are fruity, simple, drink-young wines that you'll see with labels like Sangiovese di Toscana or Sangiovese di Romagna.

California varietal wines made of Italian grape varieties like sangiovese, nebbiolo or barbera are nicknamed Cal-Ital wines.

Sauvignon Blanc/Fumé Blanc
Sancerre, Pouilly-Fumé, Bordeaux Blanc, Graves, Entre-Deux-Mers

Mediocre sauvignon blanc is a sort of generic white wine. At its worst, it can be so tart it makes you wince. Some of sauvignon blanc's characteristic aromas, like dill, grass, asparagus, green beans and bell pepper, are pleasant in small amounts, yucky when they're over the top.

But when it's good, sauvignon blanc (*SO-veen-yawn BLAHNK*) has delicate aromas of citrus, flowers, fresh-cut grass, peaches and herbal tea. If made carefully, it will show the qualities of the place it's grown, especially in flinty or chalky mineral aromas. When its acidity is balanced with fruit, sauvignon blanc has an obliging personality that makes it one of the best partners for many foods, especially dishes with pronounced salty, spicy or acidic elements.

In France, sauvignon blanc is mainly grown in two regions, Bordeaux and the Loire Valley. In Bordeaux, it is usually blended with semillon and often aged in oak, making smooth, medium-bodied wines. In the Loire Valley districts of Sancerre (*sahn-SAYRE*) and Pouilly-Fumé (*pwee-yee few-MAY*), sauvignon blanc is another creature altogether. The wines are 100 percent sauvignon blanc, and the best have complex flinty, chalky, gravelly aromas mixed in with the fruit. I love these flavors, but if you prefer softer, less austere wines, you probably won't agree with me – until you sit down to a platter of ice-cold cracked crab with lemon mayonnaise, and take a sip of Sancerre.

Back in the seventies, Pouilly-Fumé was quite the vogue, although in those B.V.C. (Before Varietal Consciousness) days, I doubt many people knew they were drinking sauvignon blanc. A souvenir from that era lingers in the use of fumé blanc (*few-may BLAHNK*) as a synonym for sauvignon blanc.

The story goes that Robert Mondavi, one of the great wine marketers of all time, wanted to improve sales of his sauvignon blanc. Taking advantage of then-current enthusiasm for Pouilly-Fumé, he labeled the wine fumé blanc. From the beginning, the two terms have been used pretty much interchangeably on labels, although American winemakers often call their oak-aged wines *fumé blanc* (à la Mondavi), and those without oak aging *sauvignon blanc*. You can't rely on this distinction, however, so read the back label of the bottle or ask your wine merchant about the wine style.

Over the last few years, wine lovers have started to get excited again about sauvignon blanc. Some folks have chardonnay fatigue and want to branch out to wines that harmonize better with meals. And the arrival of sauvignon blanc from New Zealand – vivid, complex, full-bodied wines, quite different from the French model – has changed a lot of minds about what the grape can do.

Semillon
Sauternes, Bordeaux Blanc, Graves, Entre-Deux-Mers

Semillon (*SEM-ee-yawn*) is primarily a blending grape, often recruited to round out the sharp edges of sauvignon blanc, especially in the white wines of Bordeaux. Some fine, full-bodied varietal semillon is made in Australia, and you'll also see semillon from Washington. The Australians got the bright idea of blending the grape with chardonnay, creating an easy-drinking, medium-bodied wine often called Sem-Chard, which is also made in Washington.

Even if semillon were used for no other wines, it would amply justify its existence, in my opinion, by being the primary grape in the heavenly dessert wines of Sauternes.

Syrah/Shiraz
Hermitage, Côte-Rotie, Crozes-Hermitage, St.-Joseph, Cornas

Whether you call it syrah (as in France and the United States) or shiraz (as in Australia), this grape is a winner, making robust and flavorful wines tasting of black pepper, berries, plums and black cherries, and sometimes leather and earth.

The world's benchmark syrahs – big, luxurious wines that need years in the cellar – come from the northern Rhône Valley of France. The most distinctive are the rare and costly Côte-Rotie and Hermitage, both small appellations on the steep, stony banks of the Rhône.

The arrival of inexpensive Aussie shiraz in the United States has been a boon for lovers of assertive, tasty red wines at reasonable prices. The most widely planted red grape in Australia, shiraz is made in medium- and full-bodied styles, and often blended with other grapes like cabernet and grenache. Many of these satisfying wines are available at around $10.

Not all Australian shiraz is mass-market wine. Some outstanding producers turn shiraz grown on old vines into exceedingly intense, concentrated wines.

Essentially, quality only exists if it is desired, sought after, patiently waited for; it is not a free gift.

– Emile Peynaud,
The Taste of Wine

Penfold's Grange, the greatest of all Australian wines, is largely shiraz, extremely collectible and very expensive. Originally called Grange Hermitage in homage to the great Rhône district, the wine was first made in 1955 by pioneering winemaker Max Schubert. The so-called experts weren't enthusiastic at first. One described Grange as "a very good, dry port, which no one in their right mind will buy – let alone drink," while another called it "a concoction of wild fruits and sundry berries with crushed ants predominating."

Two years after Schubert's first vintage, the head office at Penfold's told him to stop making it because this wild experiment was damaging the company's reputation. Yet Schubert kept making the wine in secret, and within a few years his critics realized that a world-class wine was born. "Hermitage" was removed from the label when the French objected to its use on a non-French wine.

During the 1980s, some American winemakers became convinced that the Mediterranean grape varieties of southern France were more suitable for California's climate than cool-climate varieties like pinot noir or chardonnay. Planting syrah, grenache and other Rhône grapes, this group soon became known as the Rhône Rangers. It was not until the second half of the 1990s that enough varietal syrah was made in the United States to make an impact on the shelves.

Inexpensive, varietal French syrah from the Languedoc region is also available.

Petite Sirah

For as long as I can remember, the wine gurus said that petite sirah, a robust red grape found almost exclusively in California, was unrelated to the Rhône Valley's syrah, notwithstanding the similarity in their names. (Some wineries even spell it petite *syrah*.) Then, lo and behold, DNA testing revealed that petite sirah is genetically identical to a Rhône Valley grape called *durif*, which is very closely related to syrah. Talk about a paradigm shift. Most of the durif in France has been replaced today by syrah, which is considered the more valuable grape. Thus, an important hunk of France's genetic heritage is conserved in the vineyards of California.

There's nothing petite about "petite," as it's affectionately called by a loyal cult of winemakers and consumers. The wines run the gamut from big to bigger. Petite sirah's trademarks are a deep, almost black color, intense plum and blackberry fruit and substantial tannins, usually enhanced with a generous dollop of oak aging. Once widely grown in California to blend with other, less hearty, grape varieties, petite sirah went out of style and almost disappeared, but now it is prized as a varietal wine.

Viognier

Condrieu, Château Grillet

Viognier (*vee-own-YAY*) is an up-and-coming glamour grape in the United States. In France, it's the primary grape in two Rhône appellations, Condrieu (*cawn-dree-YOU*) and Château Grillet (*gree-YAY*). Ideally, viognier is a light-bodied wine scented with peaches, apricots and flowers. Winemakers in California and southern France are now releasing some inexpensive, varietal versions.

Zinfandel

When it comes to capital-R Red capital-W Wine, I think of zinfandel, California's trademark red. Long the most-planted red grape in California (though soon likely to be overtaken by merlot), zin can be absolutely delicious, packed with the sunny flavors of raspberry, plum, blackberry and black cherry, complemented by the tobacco, cedar, and vanilla aromas of oak aging. It can also be very alcoholic and tannic, depending on how it's made.

Zinfandel is a *vinifera* grape like merlot, riesling and others imported from Europe. It was popular in New England in the 1830s and was brought to California in 1852, according to wine historian Charles L. Sullivan. However, Europe has no grape with the same name, so zinfandel's origin was a long-standing mystery. It wasn't until 1967 that an American plant pathologist visiting southern Italy spotted a grape called *primitivo*, which he thought looked like zin. In 1994, DNA fingerprinting confirmed that the grapes are identical.

> *A few miscellaneous red varieties*
>
> Dolcetto (*dole-CHET-toe*), grown mostly in Piedmont, makes light-bodied reds. Barbera (*bar-BARE-uh*), also from Piedmont and grown widely in California, is more grapey than dolcetto; it's the classic carafe-on-a-red-checkered-tablecloth wine.
>
> Tempranillo (*tem-pran-EE-yo*) is a robust grape similar to cabernet sauvignon in some ways, and is the primary grape of Spain's greatest reds. Cabernet franc is lighter-bodied than cabernet sauvignon, and often used for blending in Bordeaux and for making red wines in the Loire Valley.

As you can see, facts and opinions on grape varieties are as open to interpretation as everything else in wine. By now, you may be rarin' to go to the store, buy a few bottles, and form your own opinions. Before you jump into the car, read the next chapter, so you can find a good place to shop.

Those "other" grapes: hybrids, labrusca and more

If you'd paid attention in Botany 101, you'd know that grapes are in the genus vitis. The grapes that make the great wines of Europe are of the species vinifera. However, vinifera don't thrive everywhere, as Thomas Jefferson found out when he tried to recreate the vineyards of France at Monticello.

During the early days of winemaking in the American northeast and midwest, pioneer vintners wisely planted grapes that were easily available and they knew would grow well. These were mostly species native to North America, especially labrusca, riparia and the so-called American hybrids, which are crosses between native varieties. Varieties like Concord (the classic "grape jelly" grape), Delaware, Catawba, Niagara and Dutchess are still made into sweet, strong-flavored wines that have an enthusiastic following, though they're a far cry from what most of us consider table wine today.

The grapes known as French hybrids are crosses of vinifera developed for easier cultivation, bearing larger crops, adaptation to cooler or warmer climates, and resistance to disease. Among white hybrids, you may encounter Müller-Thurgau, Seyval Blanc, Vidal Blanc and Vignoles. Red hybrids include Maréchal Foch, Baco Noir, Chancellor and Chambourcin.

Nowadays, when you can buy a jug of chardonnay in just about any convenience store, the world is full of vinifera snobs who turn up their noses at wines made from other species of grape. But if the grapes are grown well and the winemaking is skillful, French hybrids can turn into terrific wines.

I've had some delicious dessert wines made from Vignoles and excellent, full-bodied Maréchal Foch and Baco Noir. The native American grape variety Norton, grown in Virginia and Missouri, makes fine dry red wines. And I once attended a tasting where six wine experts, after much discussion, decided that a bottle of Vidal Blanc from the Finger Lakes of New York – poured blind – was a chardonnay, and a pretty good one at that.

Chapter 6

A Wine Merchant of One's Own

In which you find out how to get lots of good advice

*F*ind yourself a good wine merchant.

You might save a dollar or two by buying wine at a supermarket or discount store instead of from a wine specialist. But that can be a false economy, because if you end up with wine that you don't particularly like, you haven't spent your money well.

Buying a bottle of wine is always a bit of a risk – it's all corked up and there's no way to know how it will taste. Of course the more you learn about varieties, regions and styles, the better equipped you are to figure out what's in there, but you're still just making an educated guess. The only way to know what a wine tastes like is to taste it, or to talk to someone who has.

A good wine merchant has tasted *every* wine on her shelves, or darned close. Whether she's working in a stand-alone shop or as a wine specialist in a larger store, a wine merchant can tell you how the wine tastes in terms you can understand. That's the kind of guidance you need if you don't want to buy the same wines over and over.

Here are some guidelines for starting a beautiful relationship with a wine merchant:

Shop around for a merchant you like.

It's important to find a merchant you're comfortable talking to, especially about your budget.

Expect friendly, attentive help.

Novices fear encountering a stereotypical wine snob, but most wine merchants are unpretentious, down-to-earth and eager to share the joys of wine. If you feel patronized or ignored, shop elsewhere.

No matter what else you learn from this book, the tips here will increase your enjoyment of wine and help you spend your money more wisely.

There's no reason you should put up with service in a wine shop that you wouldn't accept anywhere else.

Show up with specific needs.

Ask for wine to go with your special lasagne, or to drink at your nephew's bon voyage party. You'll soon learn whether the merchant understands your tastes and respects your price limits.

Be reasonable.

If you know you'll need lots of attention, don't show up on New Year's Eve or Fourth of July weekend. If you do, be patient.

Check out the environment.

For the wines' sake, the indoor temperature should be a bit chilly, not toasty warm. Are the bottles protected from direct sunlight? Bottles can be standing up if the shop's turnover is reasonably brisk. (One way to tell: see how much dust has settled on the bottles at the back of the shelves.) Be sure that the vintage dates on inexpensive white wines – the kind you want to drink young – are no more than a year or two old.

Sign up for the mailing list.

Almost all wine merchants send out a monthly newsletter to let you know about tastings, good deals and what's new. Some newsletters are a hoot, and they're always stuffed with information. A number of wine merchants now have Web sites as well.

Go to the shop's free tastings.

The only way to learn about wine is to drink it. When you're at a tasting, don't hide in the corner. Ask questions – believe me, the merchant or winemaker (or whoever's pouring) would love to have someone to talk to. A good, all-purpose question is: "What kind of food would you serve with this wine?" When that runs out of steam, ask about the latest harvest or whether French oak barrels are superior to American oak, and you won't be able to shut them up.

The wine snob is practically extinct in America. He or she has been replaced by the "wine geek" (also known as a "wine weenie" or "cork dork"), who has an almost religious fervor about spreading the joys of wine.

Wine tasting classes can cost from $30 to $75 a person, but a good wine merchant will educate you for the price of a bottle of wine.

Take advantage of paid tastings.

Most shops have a couple every month, often featuring more expensive wines like Burgundy, Barolo or top-of-the-line California cabernet blends. When you consider that you could pay upwards of $40 for one bottle of similar wine, spending $12 or so to taste six or seven good wines is a wise investment for planning future purchases. You'll also have the opportunity to bounce your impressions off the merchant and your fellow tasters.

Give feedback about the wines you've tried.

If you liked something in particular, say so, and you'll be steered toward bottlings with similar characteristics. If you didn't like a wine, say that, too, and the merchant can help you figure out why so you don't get a similar wine in the future.

Buy wine by the case.

It's fun to spend a few minutes with a wine merchant putting together a mixed case of wine. In the summer I like choosing a variety of refreshing, inexpensive whites; at Thanksgiving, I'll take home a selection of light reds for the big feast and the leftovers. You'll save money too, because most merchants offer case discounts, even on mixed cases. Twelve bottles really isn't all that many – if you don't finish them in a couple of months, maybe you're not drinking enough wine.

Take the wine merchant's advice.

You can read ratings in a magazine or buying guide, but nothing beats interacting with a real live human being.

If you can't find a wine specialist you like near your home, explore buying wine over the phone or on the World Wide Web. Some suggestions on where to look are in Resources, page 103.

Chapter 7

Wines By Style

*In which a versatile new way
to look at wine is explained*

*True quality is that
which succeeds in
surprising and
moving us. It
resides in the
unique, the singular,
but it is ultimately
connected to
something more
universal.*
– André Ostertag

*J*ust as one violinist interprets a Brahms sonata differently from another, each winemaker takes the raw material of wine – the grape and the terroir – and gives it an individual interpretation. At the same time, any wine, no matter how distinctive, will have some features in common with other wines. Taken together, the differences and the similarities create *wine style*.

Looking at wine in terms of style frees you from the restrictions and ambiguities imposed by considering grape variety alone. You may never have heard of Aglianico del Vulture or Vinho Verde, and have no idea what grapes they're made of or where they come from. But if I told you that the first is a red wine in a hearty, full-bodied style and the second a white wine in a light-bodied, crisp style, you'd be able to imagine pretty accurately how they taste. Once you get to know the styles of various producers and regions, you'll know that if you're craving a creamy, full-bodied white wine, a Napa Valley chardonnay or a white burgundy will please you more than a Chablis, which is also chardonnay, but generally more tart and lighter bodied.

This chapter covers the predominant styles of white and red wines, and includes sections on sparkling wine and rosé as well. There are so many wines and so many grapes out there that it's impossible to list them all – but that's the whole point. When you get the hang of this, you'll never get stuck in the same old safe-wine rut again.

I've described each wine style several ways. On the next page is a key to the descriptions.

Wine Description Key

On the label: A subjective approach to wines in the category, including some descriptive terms often used on labels.

Typical aromas and flavors: Specific nouns and adjectives of the sort found on labels and in wine magazine reviews.

Popular grape varieties: Some of the grapes most often used for the style.

Basic elements of wine: What to expect in color, alcohol level, acidity, sweetness, tannin and oak aging.

Price range: A general idea of what the wines cost.

For the best taste: The right temperature and other serving suggestions.

What's for dinner? Suggested food combinations.

Can I open It tonight? Are these wines to drink right away or keep for a while?

Shopping suggestions: Useful tips that didn't fit anywhere else.

Wines to look for, by price: Least expensive (up to $10); Mid-priced ($10 to $20); and Getting up there ($20 and over).

In the following listings, you'll see the terms best producers and top producers, usually in reference to wines over $20. What I mean is that wines from the regions discussed are only worth the money if they come from the best wineries.

I wish I could give you an all-purpose list of producers, but it's extremely hard to do. There are a million variables – different wines are available in different parts of the country, some producers only make small amounts of wine which sell out quickly, wineries are sold and the quality changes. Consult your wine merchant for relevant, up-to-date advice.

White wines by style

Can you name two white wines besides chardonnay? If the answer is no, it's time to expand your horizons. A remarkable range of white wines is out there just waiting to be enjoyed.

An important point to remember: white wines need lively, refreshing acidity to taste good, but that can make them seem sour when they're sampled without food, at a wineshop tasting, for example.

With meals, however, the acidity becomes an advantage, brightening up food in the same way as a squeeze of lemon or a sprinkling of vinegar. Be sure to try white wines with foods before you reject them for being too tart. (Red wines are often equally acidic, but their fruit, oak and tannin keep them from tasting as sharp.)

Words like *crisp* or *fresh* are complimentary descriptions of acidity in wine; *soft* is the opposite of crisp, and when a wine is *flabby*, the acidity level is so low that the wine seems shapeless and loses its edge. Every taster has a personal tolerance for acidity, so one taster's crisp could be another's soft. The interplay between acidity and fruitiness and/or sweetness is called the wine's *balance*.

Some aromas are common to most white wines, including green or red apple, pear, lemon, grapefruit, lime, peach, apricot and citrus blossoms; in wines from warmer growing areas, add melon and tropical fruits like pineapple or mango to the list. Mineral aromas like chalk, flint, limestone or gravel are found in many white wines, especially from Europe. Oak aging is not commonly used for white wines, with the exception of chardonnay and, from time to time, sauvignon blanc.

White wines can be divided into four main styles:
- *Crisp, Light-Bodied Whites*
- *Smooth, Medium-Bodied Whites*
- *Rich, Full-Bodied Whites*
- *Aromatic, Dry or Off-Dry Whites*

Crisp, Light-Bodied Whites

Picture a table for two on a shaded terrace overlooking a whitewashed village. Under an intensely blue Mediterranean sky await a crusty loaf of bread and a platter of sliced tomatoes, black olives and feta cheese drizzled with deep green olive oil. Crystal-clear mineral water bubbles lightly in two short tumblers. A cool bottle of wine, shining with beads of condensation, stands in a silver ice bucket, open and ready to be poured.

Sorry – got carried away. But wouldn't it be great to spend summer afternoons on a terrace like that? A decent consolation prize, though, is enjoying a cool glass of a light, dry wine. The crisp, lively whites described here are made for drinking at a picnic on a lush green lawn. They're generally light in alcohol and not too assertive in taste or aroma; at worst they're bland, but at best they set off the strong, acidic flavors of seafood and warm-weather produce like ripe tomatoes.

On the label: Clean, delicate, subtle, refreshing, zesty, light, crisp, brisk, young, racy (wine geek's synonym for crisp, refers to acidity).

Typical aromas and flavors: Green apple, pear, lemon, lime, grapefruit, melon, citrus blossoms, herbs, minerals, grass.

Popular grape varieties: Sauvignon blanc, chardonnay, pinot blanc/pinot bianco, pinot gris/pinot grigio, chenin blanc; sauvignon blanc-semillon blends (traditional in Bordeaux, also found in New World).

Basic elements of wine: Light color; brisk acidity; relatively low alcohol; no oak aging (or very little).

Price range: New World wines are generally inexpensive, though it depends on variety. Old World wines vary depending on size of appellation, reputation of producer, classification of vineyard.

How they taste best: Chilled but not frosty; ideal for warm weather, casual meals.

What's for dinner? Light foods like salads, cold chicken, light cheeses, pastas with pesto or other light, quick-cooked sauces, seafood (without heavy grilled flavor), Middle Eastern foods, sushi.

Can I open it tonight? Absolutely. Drink as young as possible.

Shopping suggestions: Look for recent vintages. These wines are delicate and can easily spoil, so buy from a merchant who has not stored them in an overheated shop or a bright, sunny window.

Buying Italian whites

Most are crisp, light-bodied and dry, and they can sometimes be boringly neutral. These are definitely wines meant to be enjoyed with food, because many don't have the personality to make an impression on their own. Among the wines most likely to be sold in the United States are Orvieto, Verdicchio, Soave and Frascati.

Much of the pinot grigio available in the United States, especially the widely advertised brands, is thin, industrially produced wine. Pinot bianco can be better, because it's not pumped out by the truckload. For best quality, fragrant, well-balanced wines, look for bottlings from the Friuli and Trentino-Alto Adige regions.

Wines to look for, by price:

• *Least expensive (up to $10):* California and Washington sauvignon blanc and sauvignon blanc blends, dry chenin blanc, un-oaked chardonnay; Italian whites like Verdicchio, Orvieto, Soave, Frascati; some Alsace pinot blanc and pinot blanc blends; Entre-Deux-Mers and Graves (sauvignon blanc-semillon blends from Bordeaux).

• *Mid-priced ($10 to $20):* Italian pinot grigio and pinot bianco from regions of Friuli and Trentino-Alto Adige; Loire Valley sauvignon blanc (Quincy, Reuilly, Ménétou-Salon, Sancerre and Pouilly-Fumé); Chablis and Petit Chablis (light French chardonnay).

• *Getting up there ($20 and more):* Sancerre and Pouilly-Fumé from best producers.

Smooth, Medium-Bodied Whites

Wines in this category are the picture of moderation in every way. Grapes are ripe, but not too ripe. Flavors and aromas are intense, but not too intense. Oak influence? Yes, but not too much. Sufficient acidity, but not too tart. And as a result, medium-bodied whites are adaptable to many situations and foods.

On the label: Smooth, firm, medium-bodied, silky, fruity, creamy, elegant, subtle, velvety, crisp, lively, bright, ripe, easy-drinking.

Typical aromas and flavors: Green apple, lemon, citrus, pear; in oak-aged wines, oaky, toasty, smoky, spicy, vanilla, clove, cedar, nutty, hazelnut.

Popular grape varieties: Whatever you want, as long as it's chardonnay; better values in sauvignon blanc/fumé blanc, pinot blanc, pinot gris, semillon, chardonnay-semillon blends.

Basic elements of wine: Light straw to light gold color; moderate alcohol (12 to 13.5 percent); clean, lively but not too-tart acidity; dry; oak aging can add body.

Price range: From $8 to $10 for New World varietal wines; much, much more for white Burgundy or Chablis.

For the best taste: Serve cool but not frigid.

A wine aged sur lie has been allowed to stand, sometimes for months, on the lees – the spent yeast cells which have settled to the bottom of the tank or barrel after fermentation. Lees contact can produce a lovely, creamy-textured wine. Look for the phrases "sur lie aging" or "aged on the lees" on a label.

What's for dinner? These wines, especially the un-oaked or lightly-oaked examples, can go with just about anything that sounds appealing with a white wine; for food compatibility, remember, fruit and acidity are essential. Also pleasant for before-dinner quaffs.

Can I open it tonight? Yep, or within a couple of years, at most, of vintage date. With rare, high-priced exceptions, these are not keepers.

Shopping suggestions: You'll pay a premium for chardonnay because it's, well, chardonnay.

Wines to look for, by price:
• *Least expensive (up to $10):* Varietal labeled chardonnay from California, Australia, Chile and Languedoc (southern France). Better value and quality in richer sauvignon blanc and fumé blanc, which has softer acidity than most sauvignon blanc, and is often oak-aged. Washington and Australia semillon-chardonnay blends offer good value, and are often fruitier than straight chardonnay.
• *Mid-priced ($10 to $20):* Chardonnay labeled Bourgogne Blanc (generic white Burgundy) and Burgundy subregions like Macon, Macon-Villages and Côte Chalonnaise; chablis from warmer vintages; Alsace pinot blanc; Alsace and Oregon pinot gris. Varietal labeled semillon from Australia or Washington. Sauvignon blanc-semillon blends from Graves (Bordeaux).
• *Getting up there ($20 and over):* Top California and Washington chardonnay; Chablis from best producers; Alsace pinot gris from best producers; fine white Burgundy.

Rich, Full-Bodied Whites

If you like your white wine rich and creamy, with gentle acidity and a double scoop of butter, toast and vanilla, here you are. The category is packed with variations on chardonnay, the grape that harmonizes best with the flavors of oak aging.

An important factor affecting the taste and texture of white wines is malolactic fermentation, a secondary fermentation that turns sharp-tasting malic acid into more mellow lactic acid. The result is a softer, less tart wine that sometimes has a layer of butter or butterscotch aromas.

The winemaker decides whether or not the wine should go through "malo," also called "ML." Sometimes he'll blend wine that has gone through ML with wine that has not, to create a different balance of acidity. If you see the term on a label, you can expect a richer, fuller-bodied wine that's not too tart.

On the label: Rich, lush, creamy, complex, elegant, full-bodied, mouth-filling, fruity, ripe, spicy, smoky, toasty, buttery.

Typical aromas and flavors: Pear, peach, apricot, melon, citrus, oak, toast, vanilla, clove, spice, butter, butterscotch, toffee, cream, hazelnut, almond, mineral

Popular grape varieties: Chardonnay, sauvignon blanc, marsanne and roussane (full-bodied Rhone Valley whites), semillon.

Basic elements of wine: Medium straw to deep gold color; high alcohol (13 to 15 percent); dry; malolactic fermentation softens acidity; aging on yeast lees adds creaminess; a full range of oak flavors complements (or sometimes overwhelms) fruit.

Price range: All that flavor, texture and oak don't come cheap.

For the best taste: Serve cool but not chilled.

What's for dinner? Rich, buttery wines can work well with rich foods like creamy pastas, simple lobster or crab with butter, creamy cheeses. Crisp-skinned roast chicken is a classic. As delicious as these wines can be on their own, they're not very versatile with foods so stick to simple dishes. A wine like this should be the star of the show.

Can I open it tonight? Most of these wines can benefit from a couple of years in the cellar to mellow out the oak and let the flavors meld; however, only the very greatest white Burgundy or Bordeaux lasts much more than four or five years. Some expensive, flavor-packed New World chardonnays are touted as good keepers, but their track record is unknown. Oftentimes these wines are not released until several years after the vintage date, when they're ready to drink.

Wines to look for, by price:
• *Least expensive (up to $10):* Let me know if you find any.
• *Mid-priced ($10 to $20):* Most of the great New Zealand sauvignon blanc and chardonnay; Australian chardonnay; Pessac-Léognan (subregion of Bordeaux); California and Washington chardonnay; generic Côte de Beaune (the region that includes some of Burgundy's most exclusive appellations).

• *Getting up there ($20 and over):* If a white wine hailing from anywhere other than Germany or Alsace is priced at $25 or more, chances are excellent that it's chardonnay made in this very rich style. Chardonnay from California (Napa Valley, Carneros, Santa Barbara County, Central Coast, Sonoma); Australia; Washington. The greatest white Burgundy (including Corton-Charlemagne, Meursault, Puligny-Montrachet, Chassagne-Montrachet).

Aromatic, Dry or Off-Dry Whites

Let me introduce you to some of my favorite wines – interesting, delicious, complex and great with food. Not that I expect you to actually buy them. Some Americans have been scared away from these wines by encounters with crummy jug-wine versions. Others are convinced that they only like dry wines, period. I guess I shouldn't complain, because low demand is the reason that the prices of many of these lovely bottlings remain so reasonable.

All of the wines in this group are table wines, suitable for drinking with meals. Some are dry, others are off-dry (slightly sweet), yet they're grouped together because such vivid fruit and flower aromas can give even dry wines the impression of sweetness. (For dessert wines, see Chapter 9.) Most are light-bodied, though sweetness makes some of them tilt in the medium-bodied direction.

And now, here's a word of advice: riesling. Riesling, riesling, riesling. Good riesling, dry or off-dry, is the best food wine on the planet. Riesling swirls with a kaleidoscope of aromas, including lime, lemon, peach, melon, honey, citrus blossoms and minerals, like flint and granite. Its acidity brings foods alive. Drink it.

On the label: Fruity, perfumed, aromatic, intense, well-balanced, floral, ripe, vibrant, off-dry, medium-dry.

Typical aromas and flavors: Pear, peach, apricot, green apple, spices, lime, grapefruit, tropical fruits (passion fruit, mango, pineapple, litchi), wildflowers, almond, honey – basically the whole fruit basket; mineral, flint, chalk, petrol (typical of riesling, especially with age).

Popular grape varieties: Riesling, muscat, gewurztraminer, chenin blanc (*steen* in South Africa), pinot gris, viognier, malvasia bianca.

Some of the grapes here are also mentioned in other categories of white wines. The style depends on the region and the winemaker.

*Riesling,
white riesling,
Johannisberg
riesling – they're
all names for the
same grape.
"Johannisberg" is
being phased out
on labels in the
United States.*

Basic elements of wine: Color varies from water-white through straw and light gold (generally, the sweeter the wine, the more golden the color); alcohol can be as light as 8 percent for German riesling to over 13 percent for gewurztraminer; tangy acidity balances sweetness and complements foods; generally light-bodied, but sugar can add body.

Price range: Most are ridiculously underpriced for their quality and the pleasure they give. Some good New World wines come for less than $10; prices are highest for top German and Alsatian bottlings.

For the best taste: Chilled but not so cold that aroma disappears. Use a glass big enough to trap the aroma when you swirl.

What's for dinner? Aromatic, off-dry wines can complement many foods, from simple everyday dishes to the Pacific Rim-Latino-Caribbean-Southwest-Cajun-Thai melange of flavors that's got lots of wine lovers perplexed. A little sweetness is dynamite with spicy foods. They are interesting and complex enough to drink as aperitifs.

Can I open it tonight? Like most whites, these should be consumed when young. Some top Old World bottlings, especially riesling, age well.

Shopping suggestions: Old World wines are often more complex than New World bottlings, so spending a couple of bucks extra for something fine from Germany, Alsace or Austria is really worth it.

Wines to look for, by price:
• *Least expensive (up to $10):* Many New World wines, including dry and off-dry riesling from California, Oregon, Washington. The less expensive the wine, the more likely you'll get something that's one-dimensional or lacking the balance between acidity and sweetness that makes these wines sing. Read labels carefully or ask for advice. It would be unusual to see good quality German riesling at this price level, though it can happen from time to time.
• *Mid-priced ($10 to $20):* Few aromatic table wines cost more than $20. Great pleasure awaits in this price range from Germany, Alsace, California, Oregon, Washington, Australia, New Zealand. Look for fine riesling; Savennières (*sah-ven-ee-AIR*), a Loire chenin blanc that's usually dry, fragrant, mineral-scented and nuanced; Vouvray (*voo-VRAY*), another Loire chenin blanc in dry, off-dry and sweet styles. Some California and Languedoc viognier (*vee-own-YAY*).

• *Getting up there ($20 and over):* Top Alsatian, German and Austrian wines, with aging potential; Savènnieres and Vouvray from best producers. Hard-to-find viognier from northern Rhône appellations Château Grillet and Condrieu.

All you need to know about sparkling wine

What to call it: In everyday conversation, just about everybody calls any bubbly wine "Champagne." Officially, however, only sparkling wines made in the champagne region of France are entitled to the name. Anything made anyplace else – no matter what the label may say – is properly called sparkling wine.

What it's made from: Sparkling wine in the classic French style is generally dry, and it's made from chardonnay, pinot noir, or a blend of both grapes. *Brut* is dry (though a bit of sugar is added to some brut to take the edge off the acidity); *brut zero*, which you'll see on some labels, means absolutely dry. Brut is usually a blend; *blanc de blanc* (white of "white" grapes) is mostly chardonnay, and *blanc de noir* (white of "black" grapes) is mostly pinot noir. You can turn just about any grape into bubbly wine: the Italians do it with moscato (slightly sweet, barely alcoholic Moscato d'Asti is a treat), the Germans with riesling. The most stylish sparkler in Australia is made from shiraz – red, dry and aged in oak.

Where the bubbles come from: When wine ferments, carbon dioxide, a by-product of fermentation, makes it bubble. When Champagne is made, it is fermented once and the carbon dioxide is allowed to escape. The wine is then bottled, and a little sugar is added so that a second fermentation occurs in the bottle. Since the bottle is closed, the CO_2 can't escape and it dissolves into the liquid instead. When you open the bottle, the bubbling begins.

How you can tell what you're buying: For many years, *méthode champenoise* on the label was the gold standard, assuring buyers that the sparkling wine inside was made in the same manner as Champagne. That phrase is now disappearing because the Champagne producers are aggressively protecting their brand name. Look for *méthode traditionnelle* (traditional method) or *méthode classique* (classic method), or for a label that says the secondary fermentation took place in the bottle.

If you like Champagne's bubbles, don't wear lipstick while drinking it. Lipstick contains an anti-foaming agent that causes the CO_2 bubbles to burst.

There comes a time in every woman's life when the only thing that helps is a glass of Champagne.
 – Bette Davis

What's so great about French Champagne? At its best, it's pristine, crisp and scintillating, with delicate toasty, yeasty aromas. It's also beautiful, with trails of tiny bubbles floating through golden liquid, reflecting sunlight at a posh picnic, or candlelight at a dinner for two. Madame Bovary took her first step on the road to ruin when she sipped her first Champagne at a high-society party: "Iced Champagne was served," wrote Flaubert, "and the feel of the cold wine in her mouth gave Emma a shiver that ran over her from head to toe."

Two reasons why Champagne is so expensive: 1) Making the high-quality stuff is very labor-intensive. Secondary fermentation adds several steps to the process, and French law requires Champagne to be aged for at least a couple of years before it can be sold. 2) The Champagne makers are public-relations wizards who have positioned their wine in the marketplace like Rolex, Mercedes-Benz or Cartier.

Sparkling wine by the numbers

1150:   *number of grapes, give or take a cluster, that it takes to make one bottle of sparkling wine.*
4 to 5:   *number of bottles of sparkling wine produced by a single grapevine in a single season.*
7 to 8:   *number of atmospheres of pressure in a typical bottle of sparkling wine.*
40 mph: *speed at which a cork exits a bottle of sparkling wine.*
39 million: *number of bubbles in a bottle of sparkling wine.*

Where the sparkling wine values are: All over the place, like the United States (especially California), Spain, Australia and northern Italy (look for Prosecco, Asti-Spumante and Moscato d'Asti). In France, outside the Champagne region, sparkling wine is called *vin mousseux* (foamy wine); the chenin blanc-based sparklers from the Loire can be very good.

How to serve it: Cold but not frigid, in a flute or tulip glass, and never, never in plastic anything, *please*.

What to serve with it: You'll have more fun with sparkling wine if you get over the caviar fixation and think of it as a more delicious, less bitter version of beer for pizza, chips, sushi and spicy ethnic foods (Asian, Latin American, Caribbean).

Red wines by style

Red wines run the gamut from light-colored, light-bodied, exuberantly fruity quaffers to big, bold bruisers so deep in color that they're practically opaque. You can find a red wine to suit just about any occasion, from a barbecue on a hot summer day to an after-ski dinner at a snowbound mountain cabin.

Red wines can be divided into three major styles:

- *Fruity, Light-Bodied Reds*
- *Smooth, Medium-Bodied Reds*
- *Hearty, Full-Bodied Reds*

Fruity, Light-Bodied Reds

Light reds are about as food-friendly as you can get. They have just what it takes to harmonize with meals: an abundance of lively fruit flavors and zesty acidity, and a minimum of bitterness, astringency, alcohol and heavy oak aging. Light reds usually have less complex and intense flavors than heavier wines, which is a good thing when you want the food, rather than the wine, to be the focus of a meal. What's more, wines in this category offer some of the best red wine values.

Most light reds taste best slightly chilled, which brings out their fresh, bright flavors, yet most restaurants serve them far too warm. (Actually, most restaurants serve all reds far too warm. "Room temperature" does not mean a 72-degree dining room; the cellar of a chilly stone castle is more like it.)

If you taste a light red that seems to have lost its zest, don't hesitate to have it chilled in an ice bucket for a few minutes. Waiters may give you a funny look or two – everybody knows that reds are served at room temperature, of course – but what do you care if you have the pleasure of drinking a bottle of wine that's just right?

On the label: Fruity, ready to drink, accessible, fresh, refreshing, lively, straightforward, light, supple, soft, smooth, juicy, clean.

Typical aromas and flavors: Cherry, strawberry, raspberry, grape, flower blossoms, strawberry soda.

Popular grape varieties: Gamay noir, pinot noir, grenache, sangiovese, merlot, zinfandel. Also look for dolcetto (*dole-CHET-toe*), a light-styled red from Piedmont, in Italy.

Basic elements of wine: Light, translucent color; moderate alcohol; zesty acidity balanced by delightful fruitiness; no oak (or very little); little tannin.

Price range: Typically inexpensive. They're usually less expensive to make than bigger wines – no need for pricey new oak barrels, for example, or long aging.

For the best taste: Lightly chilled

What's for dinner? Grilled chicken, fish or meats; spicy or ethnic foods (Thai, Southwestern, Chinese, Middle Eastern), ribs. They work any time you want the fruit flavors of red wine without excessive tannin or oak.

Can I open it tonight? Absolutely. Drink these wines young, young, young, before the fruit fades.

Shopping suggestions: If you're trying to select a light-bodied red from a wine list and can't find out what the wine styles are, pick one of the less expensive reds and you're likely to get what you want.

Wines to look for, by price:
• *Least expensive (up to $10):* Grenache from Côtes du Rhône,

Pink wine for sophisticates

The white zinfandel craze has made pink wine seem unsophisticated. Ironically, though, the more knowledgeable the wine-drinkers, the more likely they are to appreciate and enjoy rosé. Once you taste good dry rosé, you'll keep buying it and drinking it too. Even high quality rosé offers excellent value for money.

Good rosés are associated with warm weather because they're refreshing, usually served chilled and often lower in alcohol than other wines. Like the fruity, light-bodied reds from Beaujolais, rosés fill a useful niche between white wines and heavier, more alcoholic reds.

Rosé and blush wines are both pinkish, but they're two different things. Rosé is the name for dry wines that have long been made in Europe, especially in the South of France. (The French sometimes call these wines *vin gris* which means "gray wine.") The term "blush" is a marketing brainstorm invented to describe white zinfandel, and almost always means that a wine is sweet.

California, Australia, Spain (called *garnacha*), Beaujolais and Beaujolais Villages (gamay noir); inexpensive California merlot and zinfandel; varietal labeled sangiovese (i.e. Sangiovese di Toscana or Sangiovese di Romagna).

• *Mid-priced ($10 to $20):* Light-bodied New World pinot noir; the larger Burgundy appellations.

• *Getting up there ($20 and over):* Very unusual. Perhaps wines from some very small producers or other bottlings interesting to collectors for some reason.

Smooth, Medium-Bodied Reds

These are the red wine classics: smooth, silky, satisfying wines that taste good with a wide variety of foods. In terms of price and quality, the medium-bodied category covers a lot of ground. Plenty of inexpensive, everyday wines can be described as medium-bodied – garden-variety California and South American merlot or cabernet,

Rosé is made in a number of ways, which do not include putting ice cubes in red wine or mixing white and red. (A guy I know swears he was offered the second option in a place called Antonito, Colorado.) Most often, high quality rosé is a by-product of making red wines. When winemakers want to make a red wine with intense flavor and color, they drain some juice from the tank before fermentation to improve the ratio of skins to juice. When that light-colored juice is fermented, you've got rosé.

Look for wines from French regions like Côtes-de-Provence (good deals) and Bandol (delicious wines, but the appellation is small and stylish, so prices are higher); Sicily; and Navarra in Spain. Several California producers make good dry rosé. Rosé is not made to be cellared – it goes over the hill fast – so look for the most recent vintage date you can find, yesterday if possible.

As far as food goes, keep the warm-weather connection in mind. Garlic, tomatoes, grilled fish, olives, olive oil, citrus and strongly aromatic herbs are features of the cuisines in many places where rosé is made, such as Provence, Sicily, California and parts of Spain.

One more thing about rosé: it's beautiful. Blush wines tend to be a neon pink color, but good rosé tends toward salmon, pale rose or coral shades that look wonderful on a table, especially in the light of a long summer sunset.

for example, and a lot of Australian shiraz. But the classification also encompasses much of the greatest Bordeaux, Burgundy, Rioja (Spain's best red) and other rare wines.

On the label: Ripe, juicy, smooth, balanced, silky, supple, firm, flavorful, elegant, round, dry, soft, accessible, generous.

Typical aromas and flavors: Raspberry, blackberry, blueberry, cherry, black cherry, plum, red currant, oak, toast, vanilla, spice, cedar, tobacco, herbal, mint, eucalyptus, coffee, bittersweet chocolate. Earth, mud, dirt, tar in Old World wines.

Popular grape varieties: Cabernet sauvignon; merlot; pinot noir (Burgundy); gamay noir (Beaujolais); Italian varietal sangiovese and nebbiolo; some Chianti and Chianti Classico (not *riserva*); tempranillo (Rioja, Ribera del Duero, other parts of Spain); syrah/shiraz. *Blends:* Cabernet sauvignon-merlot (some California Meritage, some Bordeaux); grenache-shiraz (Australia); tempranillo-cabernet (Spain).

Basic elements of wine: Dry; rich ruby, garnet and (in young wines) purple colors; moderate alcohol (12.5 to 13.5 percent). Cool-climate wines will have higher acidity and lower alcohol than wines from warm climates like Australia and California. Substantial fruitiness; young wines can be tannic; oak aging adds toast, vanilla, spice.

Price range: Plenty of less-than-$10 wines for tonight's dinner, but the sky's the limit.

For the best taste: Cool; served in big glasses poured only half-full to allow plenty of swirling and sniffing room.

What's for dinner? Almost anything other than sweet, very spicy or very light foods; as long as tannins and alcohol are moderate, these wines complement dishes of varying weights and intensities.

Can I open it tonight? Less-expensive wines are ready to drink when released; up to five years of proper storage for most; a very few (top Bordeaux, especially) have awesome track records for longevity.

Shopping suggestions: This world is very large, and you'll have plenty of choices. Be adventurous, and ask for advice.

Wines to look for, by price:

• *Least expensive (up to $10):* Varietal cabernet sauvignon, merlot, syrah from just about everywhere; generic Bordeaux; Australian shiraz, grenache-shiraz and shiraz-cabernet blends (winners for fruit and flavor); Chianti; Spanish garnacha and tempranillo; malbec and malbec blends from Chile and Argentina.

• *Mid-priced ($10 to $20):* Varietal syrah, cabernet sauvignon, merlot or cabernet-merlot blends from Washington, California. Bordeaux *cru bourgeois*; Rioja; New World pinot noir; Chianti, Chianti Classico; Italian varietal nebbiolo (i.e. Nebbiolo delle Langhe).

• *Getting up there ($20 and over):* Classed-growth Bordeaux; Bordeaux-style blends from California (also called Meritage), Washington, southern Oregon, Australia, New Zealand; single vineyard and reserve New World pinot noir; village Burgundy (Chambolle-Musigny, Vosne-Romanée, Santenay, Savigny-lès-Beaune, Fixin, among others).

Hearty, Full-Bodied Reds

Big reds are all about size and intensity. They're so deeply colored that they leave traces of red on the sides of the glass as you swirl, and so aromatic you swear you can see the fragrance wafting towards you, like a genie swirling out of a lamp.

Big reds get big for several reasons: use of deeply pigmented grape varieties; growing in warm areas where very ripe grapes result in flavorful, high-alcohol wines; winemaking that extracts the maximum amount of color and flavor from the grape skins; aging in new oak barrels. All this flavor and power makes the wines delicious when drunk on their own, but can limit their versatility with foods.

On the label: Big, hearty, powerful, intense, silky, velvety, chewy, firm, focused, ripe, complex, balanced, tannic.

Typical aromas and flavors: Blackberry, black cherry, plum, black currant, red currant, raisin, herbs, mint, chocolate, toast, smoke, oak, vanilla, spice, cedar, clove, leather, black pepper.

Popular grape varieties: Cabernet sauvignon; merlot; Bordeaux blends; sangiovese (top Chianti and California); syrah/shiraz; nebbiolo (Barolo and Barbaresco); zinfandel; petit sirah; malbec; tempranillo.

One barrel of wine can work more miracles than a church full of saints.
– Italian proverb

Basic elements of wine: Dry; deep colors, sometimes almost black; high alcohol (13.5 to 15 percent); acidity less apparent under intense fruit and big, chewy, sometimes astringent tannins.

What are Supertuscans?

Supertuscans are red-wine blends from Tuscany. They combine sangiovese, the traditional red grape of Chianti, with varieties like cabernet sauvignon, merlot or syrah. Each winery gives its Supertuscans proprietary names, like Antinori's Tignanello and Sassicaia. This category of wine is wildly stylish, and prices start at around $40.

Price range: At the low end, you'll find rough-and-ready wines, many of them blends, from southern Italy, Chile, Spain, California; at the stratospheric end, collectors' wines like California cabernet sauvignon and blends, Bordeaux, Burgundy and Supertuscans. In general, the less expensive wines come from regions where the weather is reliably sunny (southern Italy, Languedoc, Chile, Australia, California); the most expensive come from cool regions (Bordeaux, northern Rhône, Piedmont) in warm, ripe vintages.

For the best taste: Cool (around 65 degrees) but not cold. Pour small amounts into big glasses and swirl a lot, because these wines soften up and offer some of their best flavors as a meal progresses. The high alcohol can make them especially warming winter wines.

What's for dinner? As far as pairing up with food is concerned, big reds can be tricky, because their high alcohol, big tannins, substantial oak aging and brawny flavors aren't necessarily food-friendly. Common pairing recommendations include dishes like robust stews, meat-sauced pastas and barbecued ribs – essentially, anything with enough fat to tame the tannins. But people who love these flavor-packed wines drink them with many foods. Sometimes a wine is so big, it seems like a meal in itself.

Can I open it tonight? Rough tannins will smooth and soften over time, but inexpensive wines may lose their fruit and end up dull. Don't just park wine in the cellar; buy a case and open a bottle from time to time and then drink it up when it tastes good. The greatest Bordeaux, Supertuscans, Rhônes and New World cabernets, merlots and syrahs can live and change for decades.

Shopping suggestions: Southern Italy is my favorite source of big reds with lots of personality for ridiculously low prices.

Wines to look for, by price:
• *Least expensive (up to $10):* Southern Italian reds pack a big punch (Aglianico del Vulture, Salice Salentino and other regions on toe and heel of boot; Sicily); cabernet and malbec blends from Argentina and Chile; California blends of several grapes (often including zinfandel, barbera or petite sirah).
• *Mid-priced ($10 to $20):* California zinfandel; cabernet and cabernet blends from Washington, Oregon, South America, Australia; petite sirah from California. Big reds tend to be either cheap and rough-edged or snazzy and expensive, but there's not much in between.
• *Getting up there ($20 and over):* Best syrah from northern Rhône Valley (Hermitage, Côte-Rotie, Cornas, Crozes-Hermitage, St.-Joseph) Châteauneuf-du-Pape (southern Rhone blend of grenache plus up to a dozen other varieties); best classed-growth Bordeaux from ripe vintages; *premier cru* and *grand cru* Burgundy from ripe years; Barolo and Barbaresco.

For more information on French wines, see Chapter 11, Cruisin' Through the Crus.

Chapter 8

Food and Wine

In which you learn how to create food and wine synergy, and why wine is better than Pepto-Bismol

> *Food without wine is a corpse; wine without food is a ghost; united and well matched they are as body and soul, living partners.*
> – André Simon

astronomic gurus talk about the marriage of wine and food as if there's an ideal wine mate somewhere for each and every food. Frankly, you'll be a lot happier if you look at food and wine pairing as a one-night stand instead. Most wines taste pretty good with most foods, so there's no need to get anxious about what goes with what. The best advice I've ever heard on this subject comes from Harvey Steiman, who writes for the *Wine Spectator*. Harvey says, "Drink wine you like with food you like."

If you'd like to take Harvey's advice as your mantra, you have my permission to skip the rest of this chapter.

Who, what, when and why?

You'll drive yourself nuts if you start thinking about how many thousands of wines are out there. In reality, you can narrow down your choices pretty easily just by thinking about factors like the people, the place, the season of the year and the feeling of the meal itself. This sounds more complicated than it actually is.

Are you having brunch or a late supper? Sitting on a sunny patio with your honey in midsummer, or toasting by the fireplace together in your fuzzy slippers? Serving 20 Thanksgiving guests who probably drink a glass or two a year, or four dedicated wine-lovers? Planning a pull-out-the-stops, spare-no-expense dinner, or spontaneously getting together with friends for a take-out pizza? Even if you're not a wine expert, I'll bet you can generally describe the sorts of wines you'd enjoy in these situations.

Choosing which wine to drink is not much different than choosing which food to eat. Just as a hearty beef stew doesn't sound very appetizing to most people when the mercury hits 90 degrees, a heavy red wine may not taste too good in hot weather. You wouldn't spend two days cooking a gourmet meal and serve it on paper plates, and you probably wouldn't open an expensive, subtle Burgundy with spicy Chinese take-out.

If your vegetarian niece and her husband are coming to dinner, you won't roast a rack of lamb; if you know that they drink sweet white zinfandel most of the time, it wouldn't be very hospitable to serve them a lean, mean sauvignon blanc. See what I mean? (But if you're craving beef stew in August, you'd probably have some anyway, and you should feel free to choose the wine you want as well.)

Flavors that cooperate, flavors that clash

Anybody who's been to a winemaker dinner, where a special menu has been created to harmonize with special wines, has heard a chef say something like, "As a side dish with the seared venison on a bed of crisp-fried jicama, I made a compote of wild blackberries and truffles to pick up the blackberry and mushroom notes in the zinfandel." That's fine and dandy for *him*, but I don't think I've ever found myself in my kitchen wondering whether the syrah has scents of *black* pepper or *white* pepper so I can decide which one to use. Chefs have the time to think deeply about *every* nuance of wine and food. At my house, dinner's practically on the table before I trot down to the basement and unearth something to drink.

Besides, a whole raft of physiological and cultural variables guarantees that a person's reaction to a given food and wine combination will be unique to her alone. For an approach that takes individual differences into account, try looking at the basic flavors in foods, the basic flavors in wines, and how they interact. The five basic flavors of food are salty, sweet, acidic, rich/fatty and spicy/hot. The five basic flavors of wine are acidic, sweet and/or fruity, tannic and/or bitter and alcoholic (usually perceived as "hot").

Conventional wisdom says that wines show off to best advantage with simple, subtly flavored dishes.That's excellent advice if the focus of your meal is the wine. I'm not likely to take a bottle of expensive merlot I've been hoarding for five years to the local Indian buffet, because the lively flavors and zingy spices of a curry are sure to zap any nuances in the wine. But most of us look at wine as an accompaniment or

For a more complete explanation of the basic wine flavors, see Chapter 2, How to Taste Wine.

To experience the flavors, do the Tea Tasting, page 109.

partner to foods, not the other way around. Since I much prefer wine to beer – the default beverage for "ethnic" anything – I'll look for a crisp, refreshing bottling to go with my tandoori chicken.

Of all the words written about wine, the ones least useful to its enjoyment are those about pairing it with food. I base my choice of wine on what I want to drink rather than on the food being served. In other words, I think wine should be matched to the person drinking it rather than the dish on the table.

Would I drink red wine with fish? Absolutely.

When would I drink a complex, profound, mature Barolo, and when a light, young, juicy Valpolicella? Whenever one or the other is what I feel like having.

What wine would I serve with oysters or smoked salmon or caviar? None. Iced vodka or very cold still water would be more agreeable.

What about dessert wines? Enjoy the wine first – or, even better, keep the wine and send the dessert back.

– Italian wine expert Victor Hazan

Finding your flavor synergy

To explore how wines go with foods, and vice versa, you can set up a simple tasting at home.

Let's say you want to see how several different white wines interact with food. There's no need to buy expensive wines for this project, and definitely don't choose more than four or five, because all the different flavor combinations will cause palate panic. For the same reason, avoid serving elaborate foods. Complicated dishes have so many flavors that it's hard to tune in on what makes a combination work.

You could choose among riesling (dry or slightly sweet), sauvignon blanc (a tart Sancerre, a wood-aged California fumé blanc, a big tropical fruit-filled New Zealand sauvignon blanc), pinot gris (richer style from Alsace, leaner style from Italy), chardonnay (a lean Chablis, a rich, oaky California or Australian chardonnay), and maybe a dry sparkling wine.

Assemble a simple plate of "tastes" for each participant:

- a lemon wedge (for acidity)
- a few salty almonds or hazelnuts, or a slice of prosciutto (for saltiness)
- a plain butter cookie or a wedge of sweet apple (for sweetness)
- a spoonful of spicy salsa (for spiciness)
- a simple creamy cheese, like a Brie or Camembert, or even a cube of plain old American cream cheese (for creamy, mouth-coating fat). If there's a good French cheese shop in your community, try my favorite, triple-cream St. André.

Each participant should have pencil and paper, a glass of water and a few slices of plain French bread to provide a buffer between the tastes.

Before you put the plates on the table, instruct everyone to try the wines without food. Suggest that they jot down reactions to each wine so they can later see if their opinions change when food is added to the equation. Some people like to rank wines on a scale of 1 to 10, with 1 being "yuck" and 10 being "yum."

Now for the fun. Distribute the plates you've prepared and try each wine with each food. Some questions to consider: How does the food change the wine, and how does the wine change the food? Do flavors become stronger or milder? Trying a wine with a food can highlight an aspect of the wine you hadn't noticed, and vice versa.

For example, if an acidic food, like a salad with vinaigrette dressing, is eaten with a sweet wine, the salad will seem even more acidic. (Imagine swallowing a mouthful of honey, and then washing it down with pure lemon juice.) The reverse is also true: Sweet foods almost always make acidic wines taste even more tart. Spicy foods tend to increase tasters' perceptions of bitterness and alcohol in wine, which is why most people prefer lower-alcohol wines (especially white wines without bitter tannins) with spicy foods. Young, tannic reds often taste great with rich, fatty meats, because fat tends to decrease the perception of bitterness and astringency in a wine.

Did you change your opinion of any wine when you tried it with food? You can stick to one wine and taste all the foods, or stick to one food and taste all the wines – your conclusions may be different depending on your approach.

If you're interested in cooking and experimenting with wines and foods, check out the menus with wine that appear in almost every issue of the Wine Spectator. *The recipes are simple, savory and accurate, and the wine suggestions are imaginative and reasonably priced.*

Look at the cause-and-effect relationships from as many angles as you can, and make notes on the combinations you'd like to incorporate into a meal in the future. Talk it over with the group, and see if different people came to different conclusions. (Believe me, they did.)

You can do a similar tasting with red wines or a mix of reds and whites. For reds, you might replace the apple with some dried cherries or a small chunk of very bittersweet chocolate. A slice of rare roast beef works well, and you can try stronger cheeses, like good Italian parmigiano-reggiano or French Roquefort. You can stage the whole thing with simple foods from the supermarket or deli. Dessert wines are another option, using flavors like vanilla, peach, apricot, raspberry, caramel, coffee and chocolate, both milk chocolate and bittersweet.

More fun and games

Another way to play with food and wine combinations is to make a favorite dish, like your special meat loaf, roast chicken with garlic or spaghetti with Grandma Luisa's tomato sauce. You'll get the most out of this experience if you make a homey dish that you eat fairly often, not an elaborate gourmet creation – unless that's the way you normally cook.

I often serve a couple of different wines with dinner when friends join us. I've got lots of wineglasses so I can put two or three on the table for each person. You can buy a case of plain, functional wine glasses at any restaurant supply outlet for very little money, and you'll use them more often than you think.

Invite some friends over to "help" you with this project. (They won't complain, I promise.) Go to the wine merchant, tell her what you're planning, and have her help you choose three or four wines that could work with the food. The bigger contrast in styles you get, the better. For example, with the meatloaf you might try a fruity, light-bodied Côtes du Rhône, an aged Spanish Rioja, and a Washington merlot-cabernet blend with lots of fruit and tannin. Another approach is to tell your friends in advance what the main course will be, and ask each of them to bring a wine that might harmonize.

Taste the wines separately before dinner, noting your reactions, and then proceed with a nice meal. Pay attention to the different combinations, and see which you enjoy most.

Sulfite anxiety

It's a funny thing about warning labels: even if you never considered worrying about something, a warning label can make you fret. "Contains Sulfites," for instance, on wine bottles, immediately makes sulfites seem dangerous, even to people who have no idea what a sulfite is.

Sulfites is the catch-all name for a group of sulphurous acids which have been associated with the cleanliness and preservation of food and wine since the time of the ancient Egyptians. That's thousands of years. So what's the problem?

According to the United States Food and Drug Administration, about 10 percent of Americans are asthmatic; up to 5 percent of those (in other words, one-half of one percent of the total population) could have a dangerous reaction to sulfites. Most seriously at risk are asthmatics who take steroids, a group of roughly 500,000 people in the U.S. Severe sulfite reactions can be life-threatening, so most steroid-dependent asthmatics have already been alerted by their doctors about the foods and beverages they should avoid.

Wine is by no means the only food that contains sulfites. Many dried fruits (apricots, peaches and golden raisins, for example), bottled lemon and lime juice, grape juice, wine vinegar, fruit toppings and maraschino cherries all contain considerably more sulfites than most wines, some more than *twice* as much.

In winemaking, the most important of the sulfites is sulphur dioxide (SO_2), which is used for preventing oxidation of newly picked grapes, and for killing bacteria and other substances that might interfere with successful fermentation. Since an excess of SO_2 can make a wine taste and smell unpleasant, any competent winemaker tries to keep sulfite use to a minimum.

Making wine without adding any sulfites at all is possible, but such wines can brown quickly from oxidation or spoil in the bottle because of bacteria or undesirable yeasts. If you are thinking of buying a wine labelled "sulfite free," make sure it's fresh from the winery.

A number of wineries grow their grapes organically, but that doesn't mean the wines are free of sulfites. As of 1999, there are no officially recognized guidelines for making organic wine. As far as pesticides are concerned, they are rarely used on wine grapes. The main use of pesticides is to keep fruits like apples and berries looking good for the supermarket, but the appearance of wine grapes doesn't matter.

In a 1995 study at the University of West Virginia, wine was found to be even more effective than bismuth salicylate (the active ingredient in Pepto Bismol) against bacteria responsible for food poisoning and other digestive-tract ailments.

Now, some bad news: you can't blame that woozy, morning-after feeling on sulfites. It's just a hangover, and it will eventually go away, although perhaps not as quickly as you'd like. Doctors propose several causes for hangovers, including the dehydration and low blood sugar that follow drinking too much alcohol. A hangover may even be caused by a brief alcohol withdrawal reaction.

Drink wine, says fitness guru

Long before Richard Simmons and Jane Fonda, there was Jack LaLanne, television's original fitness guru, a bouncy bundle of muscle and energy in a stretch jumpsuit. The Q and A below is an excerpt from an interview that LaLanne, then 81, and his wife, Elaine, then 70, gave the San Jose Mercury News in 1996.

Q: Do you have a secret food sin?

A: No.

Q: Not even one? Not coffee?

A: I've never had a cup of coffee or tea in my life.

Q: Elaine, doesn't he have any food secrets?

A: No. Believe me, he is the most disciplined person I've ever met when it comes to eating habits. He will not eat between meals. He will not eat hors d'oeuvres.

Q: (to Jack) Do you worry that people might catch you someday with a piece of cake?

A: Listen, my life's an open book. The only thing people might say we're disobeying, we like to have a glass or two of wine when we go out to dinner. And I'd rather see you drink wine than Coke or whole milk. Think about it, when you think about wine, it's one of the best foods you've got. Man has to have something, right? A little recreational something? But if you're going to have a glass of wine, make sure you have it when you eat.

Chapter 9

No-Guilt Desserts

In which you discover new treats for your sweet tooth

"Y̶ou could dilute it by half and still receive its message," wrote Hemingway in his Paris memoir, *A Moveable Feast.* He wasn't writing about a dessert wine, but he could have been. Dessert wines seduce with satiny textures and aromas like peaches, apricots, honey, mango, roses and burnt sugar. Once you've sipped one with something simple like buttery pound cake, crème brulée or peach pie, you'll never be the same.

Several means, same end

Most dessert wines are made from grapes customarily used for white wines. (Red grapes' assertive flavors and tannins work better in fortified wines.) Riesling is a classic, semillon is used in Sauternes, and chenin blanc makes some succulent wines in the Loire Valley. Gewurztraminer and muscat are frequently made into dessert wine as well. The typical flavors and aromas of the grapes are concentrated and exaggerated in dessert wine, so riesling's slight peachiness becomes incredibly fragrant and intense, and gewurztraminer's hint of rose petals can turn into a whole rose garden.

Dessert wines are crafted by several different methods, all of which remove moisture from the grapes and concentrate the sugar and flavor.

Late harvest wines are made from grapes that hang on the vine for some time after the normal harvest, ripening in the sun until they're almost raisin-like, when they're picked and pressed.

Botrytized (BOT-tri-tized) wines are made from grapes that have been attacked by botrytis bunch rot, a nasty-looking mold that shrivels the grapes and adds tantalizing and complex flavors to the wine. Botrytis is

Beuvez toujours, vous ne mourrez jamais. (Keep drinking and you'll never die.)
– Rabelais

called *noble rot* in English, probably because of the magical effect it has on grapes. In some damp, foggy regions of the world, botrytis infects the grapes almost every year; its honeyed flavors are essential to the splendid wines from the Sauternes region of Bordeaux, and the greatest sweet wines of Germany. When weather conditions are right, botrytis can attack grapes in regions where it is not a usual occurrence, adding extra layers of flavor to late harvest wines.

Ice wine is made in two different ways. Traditional ice wine is made in Germany, where it is called *eiswein*. In suitable years, grapes are left unharvested into November or even December, until they freeze on the vine. Pickers bundle up in warm clothes and head for the vineyard before dawn, where they pick the grapes by hand. The harvest is then pressed while frozen, so the water in the grapes remains ice crystals, and the tiny, tiny trickle of juice is pure flavor.

With few exceptions (Ontario and the Okanagan Valley of Canada, the Finger Lakes of New York and, sometimes, the Columbia Valley of Washington), North American wine regions are not located far enough north for grapes to freeze on the vines. Instead, a number of vintners make "icebox" wine by freezing and pressing ultra-ripe grapes, which are sometimes botrytised. These wines can be delicious, and they are far less expensive to make than German *eiswein* because you needn't wait for perfect weather conditions and then drag a bunch of high-paid Europeans out into the cold for harvest.

Dried grape wines is a catch-all category for wines made by picking ripe grapes and letting them dry out and shrivel into virtual raisins before pressing. Several different techniques are used. In France, a type of sweet wine is called *vin de paille* (straw wine), because the grapes are spread on straw mats to dry in the sun. When Tuscans make *vin santo* in the traditional way, grapes are spread out to dry on shelves in a warm storage sheds and often misted with water in hopes of encouraging botrytis. Few North American vintners make dried grape wines.

It's not just the sugar

Sweetness is the most obvious taste in dessert wines, but it's hardly the whole story. The key to the best wines is the balance between sweetness and acidity. To see what I mean, imagine a glass of plain iced tea. If you stir in a couple of spoons of sugar, the tea will taste sweet; the sweetness may even be unpleasant if you've added too much sugar for your taste. However, if you then squeeze in half a lemon, the tea will taste far less sweet, even though the amount of sugar hasn't changed. That's a simple example of how acidity balances sugar.

Residual sugar, abbreviated R.S., is the technical term for the measurement of how much sugar remains in the wine after fermentation. Dry wines contain no residual sugar, or so little that most people can't taste it. Sometimes you'll see a residual sugar measurement (written as a percentage, like 2.5 percent, or in grams per liter, like 25 g/l) on the label of a sweet wine, although it's not required by law.

But here's the catch: even if you know the R.S. of a wine, you won't be able to predict how sweet the wine will taste. A wine with fairly low residual sugar, say 2 percent, may taste cloying if it doesn't contain sufficient acidity. But when a winemaker achieves an equilibrium between sweetness and acidity, even a wine containing as much as 15 percent residual sugar tastes complex, feels lively in your mouth, and finishes clean and refreshing.

A dessert in itself

Dessert wine, with its creamy textures and complex flavors, makes a satisfying dessert in itself. And, unlike most sweets, dessert wines contain neither a crumb of cholesterol nor a fragment of fat.

When it comes to matching the wines with food, there are two absolutely contradictory theories on the best approach. According to Theory One, the dessert served must be sweeter than the wine. The idea here is that a sweeter dessert will highlight the wine's acidity, making it seem livelier and more refreshing.

According to Theory Two, the wine should always be sweeter than the dessert, which supposedly keeps the dessert from tasting too heavy and one-dimensional. For myself, Theory One does the trick more often than Theory Two, but I've also enjoyed dessert wines with foods like fresh apricots or berries, which are definitely more acidic and less sweet than the wine.

Sweet foods needn't be the only matches for sweet wines. The French serve Sauternes with melt-in-your-mouth foie gras. Salty, creamy cheeses like Roquefort, quiche with bacon and caramelized onions, and a handful of toasted hazelnuts have all been successes. During the Victorian era, late-harvest wines were regularly served with

I am tired of food moralists who tell you what you should eat. A cod liver oil pill is no substitute, either esthetically or medically, for a nice fat herring.
– Clarissa Dickson-Wright

raw oysters, a combo that sounds a bit strange today. In any case, a bright, zingy acid level is essential in sweet wines that are served with foods, whether the dishes are savory or sweet.

Shopping and splurging

Few dessert wines are truly inexpensive; you can expect to pay at least $10 for a half bottle, and some of the big names are much more costly. On the other hand, a two-ounce serving (in contrast to five ounces for a dry wine) is sufficient for almost anyone, which makes a half bottle enough for five or six people.

A number of American producers make late harvest wines, and many terrific and inexpensive dessert wines come from Australia, where they're known as "stickies." New Zealand's dessert wines, especially rieslings, are worth trying if you can find them. Some dessert wines are made in such small quantities that they're only available in tasting rooms, so keep your eyes open when you're visiting wineries.

Dessert wines are the most long-lived of white wines, due to their high sugar and acidity, both of which preserve wine. The highest quality bottlings can continue to taste fabulous for a century.

If you'd like to splurge on dessert wine, you'll have lots of choices. Château d'Yquem (*dee-KEM*) is the most celebrated producer of Sauternes (*saw-TURN*); a bottle of d'Yquem usually costs hundreds of dollars. A number of fine Sauternes are available at real-world prices, too.

Late harvest riesling, gewurztraminer, pinot gris and muscat are specialties of Alsace. The French for late harvest is *vendange tardive,* which you will see on the label. Wines from Alsace affected by noble rot – botrytis – are labelled *sélection des grains nobles.* Don't worry about pronunciation: aficionados refer to these as VTs and SGNs.

In Germany, where wines are classified by the ripeness of the grapes, dessert rieslings can be labelled *Auslese* (*OWS-lays-uh*), *Beerensauslese* (just say BA) and, for the rarest wines, *Trockenbeerenauslese* (TBA). At a wine auction in Germany during the late nineties, a TBA from top producer Egon Müller sold for about $2800 a bottle, the world record price for a newly released wine. That was an extraordinary situation, but you can expect TBAs from a good vintage to cost $50 or more, depending on the producer.

Candy is dandy but liquor is quicker.

– Ogden Nash

Counting calories

Dessert wines are far lower in sugar than many foods we consume every day. For example, a two-ounce glass – the typical serving – of a dessert wine with 10 percent residual sugar contains approximately 6 grams of sugar. At 4 calories per gram of sugar, you've got only 24 calories from sugar.

That's about the same calorie total from sugar as for two ounces of Coke Classic. A 2.1 ounce Three Musketeers bar packs 40 grams of sugar (160 calories); a two-ounce serving of Ben & Jerry's Low Fat Blonde Brownie Sundae ice cream contains 16 grams (64 calories); and two ounces of a Mrs. Fields Double Fudge Brownie offers 32 grams (128 calories). And we're not even *counting* the calories from fat. Anyway, be honest: how many times have you eaten a mere two ounces of any of this stuff? Yet two ounces of dessert wine, full of intense, complex flavors, satisfies wonderfully.

Besides sugar, the other source of calories in wine is alcohol. Most dessert wines have a similar amount of alcohol to table wine, 12 to 15 percent. Depending on the wine's alcohol percentage, just about all wines contain between 15 and 30 calories from alcohol per ounce. You can barely find a two-ounce serving of dessert wine that clocks in at more than 100 calories, total.

> *If you'd like to calculate the calories from alcohol in an ounce of wine, here's how. Multiply 163 (calories per ounce in pure alcohol) by the percentage of alcohol in the wine, which is found on the label. For example, if a wine contains 13 percent alcohol, multiply 163 by .13 to derive about 21 calories from alcohol per ounce of wine. Multiply calories per ounce by ounces of wine per serving for total calories from alcohol.*

Fortified wines

Port, Madeira and other fortified wines are rich and warming, scented with caramel, espresso, orange, almonds, hazelnuts, chocolate and plum. Thick and creamy in the mouth, their aromas can fill a room. Fortified wines get their name because they are fortified with brandy or another distilled spirit. But why did people put brandy in wine in the first place?

In a nutshell, it's because alcohol is a preservative which allowed the wines to be shipped without spoiling. Fortified wines were an early export commodity. Sherry was shipped from southwestern Spain to England and France during the fifteenth century. Port, made in the Douro Valley in northern Portugal, became popular in England during the late seventeenth and early eighteenth centuries, when French wine was unavailable because France and England were very inconveniently at war. The high alcohol content means that fortified wines keep well for at least several weeks after you open them. Due to the added spirits, fortified wines are normally 18 to 20 percent alcohol.

Fans of seafaring novels will recognize Madeira (*mah-DARE-uh*) as a Portuguese island, west of Morocco, where sailing ships took on water and supplies as they headed from Europe to South America, Africa and India. The ships bought local wine for their crews as well. Since the wines of Madeira were sour and astringent, they were doctored up with sugar, and a bucket or two of brandy was tossed in for preservation. During the long, torrid equator crossing, the Madeira mellowed into a luscious wine tasting of caramel and orange. Until the early twentieth century, the best Madeira was still sent on a cruise to the tropics and back before bottling.

Today, most Madeira is aged and mellowed in warehouses heated to 120 degrees (Fahrenheit) for several months, which is certainly simpler than sailing a square-rigger to Brazil and back. It's my favorite fortified wine, with a brilliant balance of sweetness and acidity, and lovely, complex flavors.

Only the best port in a storm

Tawny port from Australia is absolutely delicious, full of toffee and coffee flavors, and it rarely costs more than $15 a bottle.

Port is made in an array of styles, ranging from ruby and tawny, the two least expensive (usually less than $10), to vintage port (the sky's the limit). Within the European Community, only wines from a particular region of Portugal, the Douro, can legally be labeled port. The Portuguese have not managed to keep their brand name exclusive, however, so you'll also see "port" on sweet, fortified wines from countries outside Europe.

The rarest and most expensive port is *vintage port*, which, as the name implies, is made entirely from grapes harvested during a single year. Vintage port spends only two years aging in barrels because it is intended to age mostly in the bottle. Young vintage port can be so deeply colored that it looks almost black, and it tastes aggressively fruity, tannic and alcoholic, sometimes unpleasantly so. Cellar it for a generation or so and it smoothes out. Port can continue to change and improve for decades; some bottlings from the nineteenth century remain drinkable and delicious.

The Portuguese "declare a vintage" – that is, decide to produce wine in the vintage port style – only in years when producers and regional authorities agree that the wine meets certain quality standards. By the time each vintage is released to buyers, well-heeled enthusiasts are frothing at the mouth, quickly driving up prices. Many wine merchants carry a selection of vintage ports, some of them decades old.

Port is made in several other styles. From least to most expensive, the classic Portuguese styles are:

Ruby is a sweet, simple, inexpensive port that has not been aged in wood. To me, most ruby port tastes like cough syrup.

Tawny is also fairly simple but briefly aged in wood, which gives it more caramel flavors and less Luden's fruitiness. As the name suggests, it is a tawny amber color.

Vintage character (VC) resembles ruby port more than the incredibly intense vintage port implied by its name. It is made of higher quality grapes than ordinary ruby port, and aged somewhat longer before bottling.

Late bottled vintage (LBV) port is made in good years, but not necessarily the same years when a vintage is "declared" for top quality ports. LBV is the port that most closely resembles vintage port, but it's meant to be drunk within four to six years of bottling, not aged for decades.

Aged tawny, my favorite style, tastes mellower and more delicate than other ports, with aromas of caramel, coffee, chocolate and nutmeg. Aged tawny is generally labeled as 10, 20, 30 or 40 years old. However, all the wine in the bottle is not the same age. A bottle labeled 30 years, for example, isn't full of 30-year-old wine. It's a blend containing some 30-year-old wine and some younger wine.

Fruit wines: the tastes of summer

Many wine-drinkers don't consider fruit wines "serious" enough to deserve their attention. It's true that the wines don't have the complex flavors and aromas of fine grape wines, but when they're well made they're a delicious way to savor the tastes of summer all year round.

Grapes are a fruit, of course. But the term *fruit wine* refers to wine made by fermenting fruits other than grapes, like berries or pears. Technically, cider is a wine, because it is made from apples. Japanese

When they are making good port wine and the better kinds of claret and Burgundy, men act like rational creatures. In almost all their other activities we see little but foolishness and chaos.
— Patrick O'Brian, *The Thirteen Gun Salute*

saké is called rice wine, but it's actually a beer because it is made from rice, a grain.

The most important difference between making wine from grapes and other fruits is the ripeness – the sugar level – of the fruit at harvest. Fermentation is the process of yeast converting sugar into alcohol. The riper the fruit, the higher the alcohol level of the finished wine. Wine grapes can ripen until they reach a sugar level of about 20 percent of weight, which results in wine with about 12 percent alcohol.

Berries don't get as ripe as grapes. To achieve an appropriate alcohol level in the finished wine, fruit wine makers must add sugar to the crushed fruit. The amount of sugar allowed is regulated by law, and depends on the type of fruit being fermented. Besides berries, which make the best fruit wines, fruit wines can be made from pears, rhubarb, apricots – heck, if it's fruit, you can theoretically make wine from it, and somebody has probably tried. However, few fruits get remotely ripe enough to ferment without adding masses of sugar. Something like dandelion wine is really just fermented sugar-water.

A well-made fruit wine will taste like an intense version of the fruit it's made from. Although often quite sweet, fruit wines still need that essential balance of sweetness to acidity to keep from cloying.

For maximum aroma and flavor, fruit wines should be drunk fresh, ideally within a year of bottling. Since United States law does not allow labelling fruit wines with a vintage date, the only way to make sure of what you're getting is to shop somewhere that has a brisk turnover of merchandise. If your wine merchant isn't able to tell you how long a bottle has been on the shelf, find another wine merchant.

Fruit wines are best served chilled. For an aperitif, try a mixture of two-thirds sparkling wine and one-third berry wine. Berry wines are good with cheesecake or ice cream, and often shine with combinations like raspberry and chocolate.

Sherry, Baby?

The best known style of sherry in the United States is cream sherry, *a sweet after-dinner drink. Good Spanish sherry ranges from dry to sweet. The dry styles, called* finos, *have distinctive toasty scents and make flavorful aperitifs. The Spanish drink them with savory tapas. Sweet sherry styles include* oloroso, amontillado, pale cream *and* cream. *The word* sherry *is used in many countries, but the only sherry worth drinking is from Spain, and it offers excellent value for money. Ask your wine merchant to recommend the best producers.*

Chapter 10

Price and Prejudice

In which ten money-saving shopping strategies are offered

A*s a lifelong reader of Consumer Reports, I've learned that knowledge is power in the marketplace. To recognize good quality and fair prices, you need enough information to see past pretty packages and advertising hype.*

Wine may be art, but it's also a consumer product. At this point, you know enough to apply some savvy shopping strategies on your next trip to the wine merchant. Use the tips below as your guide.

1. Know your producers

A wise friend once told me that it's always better to rent the worst room in a good hotel than the best room in a bad hotel. She meant that a well-run business maintains high standards in all price ranges, while a cheap-o operation is tacky from top to bottom. Her observation applies to wineries as well.

The most consistently reliable way to buy wine is to identify producers you trust. A number of excellent wineries known for megabucks wines also produce modestly priced bottlings. Some of the less expensive wines come from larger appellations or less celebrated regions than the pricey bottlings; some are made in vintages which are less suitable for making age-worthy wines but fine for drink-it-now quaffs.

Some wineries bottle such wines under a *second label* with a different name. For instance, Mouton-Cadet, now an independent brand, began as a second label of Château Mouton-Rothschild. Château Margaux's second label is Pavillon Rouge, and Château Latour's is Les Forts de Latour.

> *Quality in wine is much easier to recognize than to define.*
>
> – Dr. Maynard A. Amerine

2. Pay attention to how the wine's made

This correlates to the tip above. From a commercial point of view, it makes sense that wineries generally lavish more costly and time-consuming winemaking techniques on their more expensive wines. Some techniques commonly used for expensive wines are:

- Picking grapes by hand, which many winemakers believe results in more nuanced, delicate wines than machine harvesting.

- Aging in new oak barrels to add toasty, vanilla oak flavors.

- Aging a white wine on the lees, which gives a creamy texture but can require stirring every barrel or tank as often as once a week.

- Laboriously sorting through grape bunches to discard moldy or unripe grapes, which is time-consuming but improves wine quality.

However, some wineries hand-harvest *all* their grapes, or age *all* their white wines on the lees, or use other expensive procedures – and when they do, they usually specify it on the label, or in tasting notes that your wine merchant can share with you. (Winery Web sites are also a great place to find specific information on how wines are made.) You're getting more complexity of flavor for your money when you can find wines that are more painstakingly made, yet lack the big price tags.

A few examples of inexpensive wines from quality producers: The Antinori winery of Tuscany produces a terrific little red wine called Santa Cristina *– it's not labeled Chianti, but it's got Chianti character. California's much-lauded Bonny Doon makes tasty blends called* Big House Red *and* Big House White *for under $10. Jaboulet, one of the top producers of pricey Rhône Valley wines like Hermitage and Côte-Rotie, makes a simple but delicious Côtes-du-Rhône called* Parallèle 45.

3. Don't be an appellation snob

Some winegrowing regions, such as the Haut-Médoc in Bordeaux, the Côte d'Or in Burgundy, or the Chianti Classico district of Tuscany have been producing fine wines for decades or centuries.

Other prestige areas may not have such lengthy records, but once they have been praised by the wine press and sprinkled with the dollars, marks or yen of collectors, their reputations are assured, and buyers pay a premium for wines hailing from those particular spots on the map. Cabernet sauvignon from Rutherford or Stags Leap in the Napa Valley is one example; merlot from Washington's Walla Walla appellation is another.

Grapes from these well-known appellations cost wineries a bundle. When a winery wants to market good quality wines which are inexpensive, it must seek out flavorful grapes from less exalted sources. Sourcing grapes from a larger area allows a winemaker to balance the flavors of grapes from one area with those from another. If a producer is reliable, it doesn't make sense to shy away from wines labeled with broad appellations like California, Bordeaux or South Eastern Australia (an appellation which includes 99 percent of Australia's vineyards).

4. Use the "just next door" approach

A border is just lines on a map. It's not unusual for winemakers in an appellation located *near* a famous and expensive district to make wines which are similar to the bottlings from the big names next door, yet lower in price because the appellation is less prestigious. Some of the greatest sauvignon blanc in France comes from the Sancerre (*sahn-SAIR*) appellation in the Loire Valley. Barely 30 miles down the road you'll find Quincy (*can-SEE*), a region that shares many characteristics with Sancerre and can also be the source of crisp, delicious sauvignon blanc. You'll pay less for good Quincy than for good – or even so-so – Sancerre, simply because Quincy does not have the same reputation. A good wine merchant will point out this kind of opportunity.

Here's one of the simplest ways to drink better for less money. As of 1998, chardonnay was the best-selling white wine in the United States and merlot was the best-selling red. As a result, prices for both wines are generally a few dollars higher than for wines of similar quality made of less popular grapes. Do yourself a favor and try some of the dozens of delicious wines made from grape varieties you've never heard of.

5. Don't be a varietal label snob, either

When a wine does not contain a minimum of 75 percent of a single grape, it can't be labeled with the name of a single grape variety. Yet some of the most interesting and delicious wines in the world are blends of several different grapes, and many are extremely well priced. You're making a mistake if you insist that every wine you buy be labeled Chardonnay or Zinfandel or whatever.

6. Non-vintage wines can be good buys

Wine with a vintage date on the label is not necessarily better than a *non-vintage (NV)* wine. In their quest to make consistent yet inexpensive wines, winemakers often blend wines from different years and come up with very tasty results.

7. Put something other than wine in your basement

Ninety-nine percent of all wine is made to drink young. Fruity, fresh wines (2 to 3 years after vintage for whites, at most 4 years for reds) almost always represent the best values. And, truthfully, a lot of people prefer the flavors of young wines to aged wines anyway. The few wines worth aging are invariably more expensive. (More on aging and cellaring wines in Chapter 12, When Age Matters.)

8. "Good and big" is less expensive than "good and small"

Well-heeled wine collectors seek out wines from small appellations and small producers because the whole point of collecting is to own something rare. But a winery needn't be small to make good wine. Bottlings from big, good-quality producers are often smart buys, because the prices haven't been enhanced by the boutique winery halo. Big producers have more sources of grapes, more flexibility in blending and often more efficient equipment for making wine, all of which can result in good wines at lower prices.

9. Dare to be different

As I've said before, there are two kinds of wine: pleasant, well-made wine that lacks a distinctive sense of place, and wine that is unique to its terroir, the place it's grown. Both are enjoyable to drink, and both can represent good values. The first category is not that hard to find if you follow the tips in this chapter. The second category is not that hard to find if you're willing to pay lots of money for wines from places like Burgundy, Bordeaux or Piedmont.

Finding wines that are inexpensive *and* speak of the earth takes more work and daring on your part, but it can be done – and I can't begin to tell you how delighted you'll be when you discover a little treasure. Your best ally is a wine merchant with a sense of adventure. Look for a shop that carries more than varietal wines and big names. Seek out wines from regions like Minervois, Corbières and Roussillon in southern France; Buzet and Cahors in southwest France; Ciró, Aglianico del Vulture and Salice Salentino in southern Italy; and Rueda and Priorato in Spain. Who cares if you can't pronounce them? You'll learn soon enough, if you enjoy the wines.

10. Ignore the wine critics

Many wine merchants can tell you about customers who taste a wine and say they like it, then look up its rating in a magazine and decide not to buy it. Just think: Rather than believe their own taste buds, those folks have decided to go along with the opinion of a person they've never met, who lives a very different life in a distant city or country, who tasted the wine in question weeks or months earlier, at the same time as he probably tasted 30 or 40 other wines, before it went through the wear and tear of being shipped to your corner store. That guy doesn't even know what the wine *tastes* like today, let alone what the weather's like in your home town, or what you're having for dinner tonight.

Even if you never bother to look at the ratings, the system still has an effect on the wines you drink. More than one winemaker has told me that he crafts wines in ways that generally impress reviewers – with a lot of oak influence, for example, or emphasizing power rather than finesse – rather than to his personal taste. Winemakers, even those who receive high scores, speak privately about their dislike of the

I do deplore the way the scores have been abused by lazy American retailers. I even took legal advice on trying to prevent retailers from using my scores as a marketing tool, but I couldn't stop them.

– Robert Parker

system, yet a high rating can be so profitable that they don't feel they can opt out of the ratings game.

Some collectors buy wine strictly on the basis of reviews and never taste any. They just hoard it to re-sell later. (I don't recommend doing this with your retirement account, by the way.) A wine merchant told me the story of a customer who religiously bought two cases of high-rated, hard-to-get merlot from a tiny Washington State winery every vintage for the better part of a decade. Once, as the man was picking up his annual order, the merchant commented that he'd been collecting these particular wines for a long time.

The customer grinned. "Yep, and I've never opened one yet," he proudly replied.

Do the ratings have any value? In a perverse way, yes: they focus attention on a very few wines and leave lots of room for the adventurers among us to make our own discoveries. There's plenty of good stuff out there if you're willing to taste carefully and come to your own conclusions. Find a wine merchant you can work with. Taste a lot of wine, and pay attention. Drink the wines you like, no matter what others say about them.

The kings of the ratings

Just about anybody who buys wine in the United States has encountered the 100-point rating system. The most influential of several publications that assign scores to wines are the Wine Spectator and the Wine Advocate. The Wine Advocate was founded by a Maryland attorney, Robert Parker, who is now the single most important wine critic on Earth. It's a newsletter jam-packed with numbers and adjectives in teeny-tiny type.

The Wine Spectator is a glossy lifestyle magazine about expensive hotels, restaurants and winery owners living in extremely nice châteaus – but anybody who says he buys the Spectator and doesn't check the ratings is about as credible as someone who says he buys Playboy and doesn't look at the pictures. When the Spectator proclaims the "vintage of the century" somewhere, or Parker anoints a winemaker with 90-plus scores, the wine collectors whip out their checkbooks and prices inflate.

Chapter 11

Cruisin' Through the Crus

In which you see how the French recognize their best vineyards

At this point in the book you must be thinking, "Isn't it time to look more profoundly at the quality designations in France, the nation that serves as benchmark and model for the wine industry worldwide? The concept of *cru* is particularly intriguing. After all, a thorough knowledge of French wine is an absolute necessity for anyone who truly wants to experience the plethora of pleasures that wine can offer."

You know, I was thinking exactly the same thing.

Didn't Elvis sing "Don't Be Cru?"

Cru is the French word for a vineyard or for the wine that comes from that vineyard. Whether it's spelled *cru* (singular) or *crus* (plural), it's pronounced exactly the same way: *crew*.

You'll see the word *cru* on many French wine labels, usually combined with another word, like *grand* (great) or *premier* (first). It's used differently in different regions, but it always has to do with a vineyard and, like everything else on a French wine label, its use is regulated by law. The most important point is that *cru* designates a wine that's considered to be – or should be, or is made of the raw materials that would conceivably allow it to be – of superior quality. When was that decision made? Is it still valid today? Well . . . it depends.

Grand cru or *premier cru* on a label does not guarantee great wine. It's the vineyard, not the wine, that merits the designation. The phrase has nothing to do with the quality of a particular vintage, the skill of the winemaker, whether the importer bothered to ship the wine in a refrigerated container so it didn't simmer in the Panama Canal, or any of the many other factors that influence the taste of the wine you pour into your glass. A *grand cru* or *premier cru* designation on a bottle does guarantee one thing, however: you'll be paying a higher price than for a wine without it.

Here's the crux of the crus, region by region.

Bordeaux

The most famous and influential wine classification that has ever been made covers two Bordeaux subregions, the Médoc (*med-DOAK*) and Sauternes (*saw-TURN* – the s is silent). In 1855, a panel of wine brokers was asked to choose which wines would be featured at that year's Universal Exposition in Paris. In the process, they devised a quality ranking system for part of Bordeaux that is used to this day.

Bordeaux is a huge region, encompassing thousands of châteaus, but only 61 at that time were considered worthy of ranking as *crus classés* (*crew class-SAY*), classed vineyards, or "growths" as they are called in English. All the red wines ranked came from the Haut-Médoc (*oh med-DOAK*) region except for one, Château Haut-Brion, which is located in Graves (*grahv*). The white dessert wines of Sauternes were ranked separately.

For red wines, the brokers decided on five classifications, *premier (first) cru*, *deuxième (second) cru*, *troisième (third) cru*, *quatrième (fourth) cru*, and *cinquième (fifth) cru*. English-speakers refer to the classifications as "first growth," "second growth" and so on. First growth is tops and the châteaus "decline" in prestige to fifth growth – but this is still a ranking of the best of the best. Any classed growth in Bordeaux is a big deal.

A first growth château can put *Premier Cru* on the label; the others can only say *Grand Cru Classé* (classed growth), so you'd have to thumb through a wine encyclopedia or ask your wine merchant to find out their precise classifications. The classification has some effect on price but not necessarily on the quality of the wine, because there are so many factors besides terroir involved.

You see, the classifications never change. If, for instance, a second growth château is sold, the château remains a second growth, even if the new owner doesn't know beans about making wine. (That's a farfetched scenario given the prices that fine châteaus sell for, but it's theoretically possible.) After several vintages under the new owner, the critics and brokers might decide that the château is not producing wine that's up to the standard of a second growth. Still, the terroir hasn't

Bordeaux calls to mind a distinguished figure in a frock coat. He enters his moderate enthusiasms in a leather pocketbook, observing the progress of beauty across his palate like moves in a game of chess.
– Frank Prial, the *New York Times*

changed, so the château remains a second growth, though it's considered an underachiever. Knowing a château's classification is interesting, but it guarantees nothing.

In the "never say never" department, there is *one* château in the Médoc that has changed its status since 1855. The original classification named four *premiers crus* (first growths): Château Lafite-Rothschild, Château Latour, Château Margaux and Château Haut-Brion. In 1973, after a tireless century or so of lobbying by its owners, Château Mouton-Rothschild was elevated from a second growth to a first growth, making five altogether – certainly the Dream Team of wine.

In the St.-Emilion region of Bordeaux, rankings for *grands crus classés* were determined in 1955 and have been revised every ten years since. They don't confer anything near the prestige of the 1855 classification, although chances are they're a more accurate reflection of quality today because of the revisions.

Since only 61 châteaus were dubbed classed growths by the wise men of 1855, the designation *cru bourgeois* (*crew boorsh-WAH*) was developed in 1932 to distinguish several hundred of the best remaining producers in the Médoc. There are several different quality rankings, but the only words legal on labels are simply *cru bourgeois*. Cru bourgeois wines are some of the best Bordeaux values today.

Burgundy

In the Côte d'Or, the most important region of Burgundy, there are only two cru designations, *grand cru* and *premier cru*, that single out vineyards which have been judged outstanding. *Grand cru* is the higher of the two.

In Bordeaux, a cru is tended by only one producer, the château which owns it. In Burgundy, however, many of the great vineyards are divided up among dozens of owners, some of whom own as little as one row of vines. It stands to reason that not all of the owners are equally skillful or conscientious winemakers. Yet every wine from that vineyard is entitled to carry the vineyard name and *grand cru* or *premier cru,* no matter who makes it. You see how quality can vary, sometimes drastically. (A few Burgundy vineyards are wholly owned by one producer. The wines from those vineyards are usually labeled with the vineyard name and the word *monopole*.)

In French, bourgeois refers to the well-to-do social class just below the aristocracy, what Americans would call upper middle class.

In Bordeaux, a wine producer is a château; in Burgundy, it's a domaine or, less frequently, a maison. In the rest of France, all of the terms are used. Wine buffs usually just refer to producers by their names, such as Latour (Bordeaux), Trimbach (Alsace) or Jadot (Burgundy).

If you want to learn about Burgundy, it isn't enough to recognize vineyard names or know the meaning of *grand cru*. Identifying the good producers is key, because so many producers can make wine from any one vineyard. When you start exploring the region, your best bet is to find a knowledgeable wine merchant to guide you through the maze. Even wine professionals turn to specialists for advice on Burgundy.

Chablis

Chablis is the northernmost part of the vast Burgundy appellation, but it is considered a region of its own. Labels from the area say *Chablis*, not *Bourgogne*. The crus are organized differently than in the Côte d'Or, which makes sense, because if there were some standardized system it might be easy for foreigners to understand, and *then* what?

Chablis includes seven grand cru vineyards, all of which are located on the same southwest-facing slope near the town of Chablis. The premier cru vineyards are classified under a number of district umbrellas; for example, in the district Montée de Tonnerre you'll find three premier cru vineyards. As in the rest of Burgundy, these vineyards can be divided among many different producers, so knowing the vineyard names alone won't give you enough buying information. This is what wine merchants are for.

Beaujolais

Like Chablis, Beaujolais is also part of Burgundy. The appellation for its lowest quality wines is Beaujolais, which encompasses a huge region. The next appellation up, Beaujolais Villages, is also extensive. The smallest appellations are the ten hill villages collectively known as the *cru Beaujolais* (*CREW bo-jo-LAY*). They have been singled out because the wines are fuller-bodied, and more age-worthy than other Beaujolais and reflect terroir in unique ways.

The cru Beaujolais are Brouilly, Morgon, Moulin-à-Vent, Fleurie, Côte de Brouilly, Juliénas, Régnié, St. Amour, Chiroubles and Chénas. Each cru is supposed to have its own distinctive characteristics.

The hitch: the words *cru Beaujolais* don't appear on labels. Instead, you'll see the name of the village but – oh those French! – sometimes they don't even put *Beaujolais* on the label. If you like these wines, you'll just have to learn to recognize your favorite village names. You could also do the same thing as many savvy wine shoppers: tell the wine steward or merchant that you're looking for a cru Beaujolais, and if there's one available, he'll point it out.

Alsace

Anyone who's traveled through Europe and visited Alsace might well have noticed some similarities between that region and Germany, which is just across the Rhine. If you're smart, however, you won't mention those observations to the Alsatians. The one time I made that mistake, I was informed that they are absolutely, definitely *French*.

French indeed, yet an almost Teutonic sense of order shows in their wine quality designations. *Alsace Grand Cru* is an appellation in itself, created in 1983, to designate wine from one of several grand cru vineyards and a single vintage. Only four grape varieties – riesling, gewurztraminer, pinot gris and muscat – can be called *grand cru*. Requirements such as smaller vineyard yields and minimum sugar levels at harvest differentiate wines labeled Alsace Grand Cru from simple Alsace.

However, as in other regions, the grand cru designation doesn't guarantee excellent wine. Some of the grand cru vineyards are considered better than others. Some of the vineyards are so large that they encompass superior and inferior growing areas, even though all the wine grown there will be labeled the same way. And there are always the issues of how the vines are tended and how the many vintners make the wines. Let the buyer beware, and get advice from a good wine merchant.

Germany's first growths

No country has a system of vineyard classification as extensive and carefully monitored as France's. Until recently, lovers of fine German riesling have had to be content with learning the names of the best producers and vineyards. However, a group of top producers from three regions, the Rheinhessen, Rheingau and Pfalz, now designate their best vineyards as Erstes Gewächs (first growths). An Erstes Gewächs vineyard has an historical tradition of greatness, and the wine is made in accordance to strict rules established by the wineries, stricter than German government regulations. A wine labeled Erstes Gewächs also carries the vineyard name.

Excuse me, which wine goes with "Stairway to Heaven?"

Marketing research has found that many people choose wines by the prettiest labels, which explains why wineries put so much time and money into package design. According to psychological researchers at the University of Leicester, in England, there's another way to influence wine purchases: background music.

At an English supermarket, the psychologists placed four French wines and four German wines, priced about the same, next to each other. Then, while shoppers browsed, French accordion music or German polka tunes were played in the background. Believe it or not, more people bought French wines when the French music played, and German music had the same effect for German wines. In follow-up interviews, however, fewer than 15 percent of the shoppers said they were consciously influenced by the music.

Chapter 12

When Age Matters

*In which the mystique of old wines is debunked
and drinking young is recommended*

*I*n my favorite episode of the defunct television series "Northern Exposure," ditzy Shelley accidentally drops a bottle of rare old wine that belongs to Maurice, the pompous ex-astronaut. To keep him from discovering that his 1929 Château Très Cher has soaked into the Alaskan tundra, she and Eve, the hypochondriac foodie, glue the bottle back together (this is television, remember) and concoct something to fill it.

Starting with a base of red jug wine, Eve sprinkles in stuff like herbs, pipe tobacco and peat moss, "for that earthy quality." Of course, at the fancy banquet where the wine is served, everyone exclaims and rolls their eyes over its wonderful flavors.

Such is the mythical power of old wine that the label alone guarantees reverence. When you read about wine auctions, or eavesdrop on wine collectors, you'll hear about aged wines and the fabulous prices they bring. Vintage Bordeaux regularly sell for $250 a bottle and more. A bottle of 1907 vintage Champagne salvaged from a 1916 wreck in the Baltic Sea sold in 1998 for $4,068. Heaven only knows whether it was drinkable, but that's not the point.

Unfortunately, all this talk makes normal people – those of us who consider a wine "aged" if it came from the supermarket last week – presume two things: 1) old wines bring the most pleasure, and 2) putting wines away in the cellar invariably improves them. As general principles, both are absolutely wrong.

At first I was depressed, but I finally hit upon a reason to celebrate. As of midnight, all the great wines are one year older!
–Lucius Beebe on New Year's Eve

Youth and age

Repeat after me: 99 percent of the wine in the world should be drunk young. Fresh, fruity flavors and aromas, which generally don't last very long, are the most appealing qualities of the vast majority of wines. "Young," for almost all inexpensive white wines and most light-bodied reds, means the most recent vintage on the market, or at most two years back. For fuller-bodied red wines, add a year or two.

Red wines are generally considered the best candidates for aging. When white wines are made, the grape skins are separated from the *must* (unfermented grape pulp) within several hours of crushing. When red wines are made, the skins are steeped with the must, remain mixed in throughout fermentation, and sometimes are left to soak in the newly fermented wine for as long as two weeks afterward, to extract as much color as possible.

Because of their long contact with the skins, red wines develop stronger, more concentrated aromas and flavors than white wines. Reds also take on tannin, the substance that can make young red wines feel rough and astringent in the mouth. Tannins act as a preservative for wine and must be present in sufficient quantities if a red wine is to improve in the cellar.

I occasionally hear from someone who has an old bottle of wine and wants to know what it's worth. The answer is, "Probably nothing." Except in extremely rare cases, auction houses and wine brokers want a case of wine, not a single bottle. In addition, an old wine's value is based largely on credible documentation of its provenance – the origin of the wine and where and how it has been stored – which is information that few non-collectors can provide.

Wines can change their character in just two or three years, especially young reds. A young cabernet sauvignon, for example, has a signature aroma of black currant, and can be so tannic that it actually feels rough in your mouth. In the best-case scenario, the tannins smooth out and the wine's texture becomes velvety. Simple fruit aromas like black currant (*cassis* in French) are joined by more complex notes referred to as "bottle-age" aromas, like cedar (also called cigar-box), leather, chocolate, mushrooms and tobacco. However, there's no guarantee that any given young red will evolve that way. Gauging a wine's aging potential is a combination of experience and guesswork.

Some people ooh and aah over thirty-something Rhônes or octogenarian port. Others consider drinking very old wines the vinous equivalent of necrophilia. One thing's certain: When a wine isn't suited to aging, or sits in the cellar too long, the fruit disappears but nothing much takes its place. Elements of the wine such as oak, bitterness, or acidity, which may have been in proportion when balanced by fresh fruit flavors, start to stick out like sore thumbs. Contrary to popular belief, over-the-hill wine doesn't taste like vinegar. It's just musty and dull.

Finding keepers

Although it would make the lives of wine lovers infinitely simpler, a bottle of wine is not like one of those Thanksgiving turkeys with the pop-up timers. There's no built-in signal that pops out of the bottle when the wine's ready to drink.

Such a device would only work if every wine had one magical moment of maturity. Even if that moment existed, how would you know when it was? In reality, a good wine tastes good at many stages of its evolution, and personal preference determines when it's "best." Storing wine to drink several years down the road is about enjoying the changes.

If you're considering buying a wine for the cellar, remember that if you don't like it now, you probably won't like it later. Wines are like people: if they're unpleasant when young, they're not likely to be pleasant when old. I'm astounded at how often I've heard someone say that he can barely choke a wine down, but he's sure it will taste better in the future because his brother-in-law/lawyer/(fill in self-appointed wine expert here) told him so.

Big-name wines from prestigious appellations are obvious cellar selections, but they can cost a bundle. *Futures* (pre-release sales) on 1996 Château Latour, for instance, sold for almost $3000 a case, and the price shot up further when the wine was actually released. That money isn't earning interest, either. To start more modestly, ask your wine merchant's advice on good candidates.

When you decide you like a wine well enough to let it take up space in your basement for years,

Red wines are most often cellared, but some white wines – generally from the Old World – also change in lovely ways if aged in the right conditions. High quality German riesling and white Burgundy or Chablis (both made from chardonnay) are possibilities. The best dry chenin blanc and sauvignon blanc from the Loire Valley are said to age beautifully, though I've never been patient enough to find out. Dessert wines can develop wonderful, honey-like flavors, and a good number, especially late harvest wines from the Pacific Northwest, California and Australia, are reasonably priced.

commit to buying at least a case, so you can taste it as it changes. Ask the seller when you should start trying it, and then open a bottle every six months or so. When it tastes great, drink it up. You'll be glad you bothered to sock it away.

Storage tips

Whether or not you've got an official wine cellar, you'll probably want to keep a few bottles on hand so you don't have to run to the wine shop every time you make dinner. It's economical, too, because most wine merchants offer discounts for case purchases.

To store wine for a month or two, it's perfectly okay to simply keep it in a fairly cool, dark place where the temperature doesn't vary by more than a few degrees. If you don't have a basement, find an interior closet or cupboard that stays relatively cool. The kitchen counter or the top of the refrigerator are *not* good spots for wine storage, no matter how pretty the bottles look in that sweet little wine rack from Pottery Barn.

As for storing wine in the refrigerator, that's okay for a couple of weeks, but eventually the corks dry out and the wines oxidize. Expensive bubbly gets this treatment a lot. By the time a special-enough occasion rolls around, the stuff in the bottle is often sour, brown and flat.

To store wine safely over the longer term, you need to protect it from excessive heat and light. A cool, dark, corner of the basement does the trick nicely, as long as it's nowhere near a furnace, hot water heater or other heat generator. The most important factor is constant temperature, which is generally recommended to be no more than 65 degrees and no less than 55 degrees. If the temperature rises a few more degrees, don't fret, as long as it warms slowly and cools slowly. Abrupt temperature swings are lethal for wine.

It has long been believed that the difference between wine stored at 65 degrees and wine stored at 55 degrees was simply that the wine stored at the higher temperature would age somewhat faster than the other.

The reality may not be so simple. Research shows that the flavors that develop in wine stored at temperatures even slightly warmer than 55 degrees may not be as desirable as the flavors that develop in wine stored at lower temperatures. If you've got a big investment in your cellar, it will pay over the long run to keep the temperature at 55 or lower.

The simplest form of wine cellar is simply stacking a few cases of wine in an appropriate spot. To move one step up, you could bolt prefabricated cabinets, backs removed, to the coolest wall of the basement, which will serve as a cooling and insulating device. If you want to spend more money, any wine paraphernalia catalog will give you plenty of pricey gizmos to choose from. Custom cellar-builders advertise in wine magazines.

If all that sounds like too much trouble, many wine merchants will store wines for you in ideal conditions for a small fee.

Part of the fun of a cellar will be the surprises in store for you, because wine is, thank goodness, so unpredictable.
– Kermit Lynch

Chapter 13

Choosing Wine for a Crowd

In which buying wine for weddings is simplified, and you have a couple of dollars left over for a honeymoon

When a big celebration comes along, wine is a necessity. But even if you often pick up a nice bottle for yourself, buying ten cases is a whole different thing. Here's how to do it right.

Keep it simple.

Pick one wine that will appeal to everybody and harmonize with the whole meal. It should be young, fruity, food-friendly and not too tart. My favorite choice for almost any menu or buffet is a light-bodied red, served slightly chilled. (At our wedding, we served a dry rosé.) If your guests aren't regular wine drinkers, a white wine with a bit of sweetness, like an off-dry riesling or chenin blanc, might please them. In any case, you needn't offer "red or white."

Don't get stressed out.

Big events are a headache already, and there's no point in letting wine make things worse. When you're buying wine for a celebration, it's comforting to remember that unless the guests are in the wine business, most of them won't even notice what they're drinking.

Keep it inexpensive.

Wine doesn't need to cost a lot to serve its most important purposes: enhancing food and creating a festive atmosphere. A friend once asked for advice on what to pour at her mother's 80th birthday party, a sit-down dinner for 200 guests, few of whom drank wine regularly. The caterer had suggested several wines that cost as much as $15 a bottle. I've got a feeling the caterer didn't appreciate it when I said that there are plenty of perfectly nice wines available for much less money. If money's no object, then popping open a couple of cases of Dom Perignon at 150 smackers a bottle is an impressive gesture. But unless you're hosting 200 wine buffs, what's the point?

Be adventurous.

There's nothing wrong with serving chardonnay or merlot if that's what you really want. However, the most popular wines will be more expensive than equally delicious wines made from less popular grapes. When you're buying a lot of wine, those dollars add up.

Try the wine in advance.

A hotel or catering company that's billing you thousands of dollars for a meal should be willing to open a bottle or two of wine for you to taste. Otherwise, go to the store, buy a few of the candidates yourself, and try them at home. Given how much the total event will cost, it's worth investing a few bucks to make sure you get a wine you like.

Know your options.

Your choice of wines may depend on where the party is held. Most hotels, country clubs and similar venues would prefer that you choose wines already on their lists, because it's easier for them, or because they have the wines in stock.

If you have a wine you prefer, you can ask the venue to order it. (You may have to insist.) In some states, it's legal to supply the wine for an event yourself as long as the venue or caterer agrees. If nothing on the wine list looks good, ask what the corkage charge per bottle would be if you bought wine elsewhere.

Consult a wine specialist.

Few caterers or party-planners know much about wine, and the banquet managers at hotels aren't much better. They usually just point customers to one or two old reliables that are easy to obtain. If you're able to buy your own wine, work directly with a wine merchant or a good supermarket wine department.

Monitor the service.

You will probably be charged based on the number of bottles opened. Unfortunately, servers at big events often open far more bottles than necessary, either for their convenience or the venue's profits. If finances are an issue, discuss your concern with the banquet manager.

When she's asked to recommend wine for a wedding, wine merchant Jean Ousterhout in Portland, Oregon, helps the bride-to-be select five or six wines in the requested price range. Ousterhout advises the bride to invite a group of friends over to taste the wines and vote on a winner. "They usually say that the tasting was more fun than the wedding," she reports.

When an event is casual, one possible solution to the problem (in states where it's legal) is instructing servers to pour wine once and then leave an open bottle of wine on each table so people can help themselves as they like.

Re-think sparkling wine selection.

A wedding or rehearsal dinner demands a sparkling wine for toasts. To make a good selection, think about when the bubbly will be served. A dry (*brut*) wine will taste best as an aperitif with hors d'oeuvres. If your menu's appropriate, sparkling wine can make a nice accompaniment for an entire meal. But if you're serving the bubbly with wedding cake or dessert, stay away from dry sparklers, which are high in acidity and will taste just plain sour. A very fruity sparkling wine – like a chenin blanc-based *vin mousseux* from the Loire Valley, or something slightly sweet, like an Asti-Spumante or Moscato d'Asti from Italy – works better with cake.

One of the tackiest things I've ever seen was a wedding where the happy couple and the wedding party drank expensive Champagne while the guests drank cheap sparkling wine. Wine merchants tell me that this unspeakably rude practice is rather common.

Yikes! Since when is it considered polite to serve your guests something of lesser quality than you serve yourself? I suppose the next helpful hint from wedding planners will be to serve the guests hamburger while the wedding party eats filet mignon.

Buy the right amount.

Once a wine is chosen, the next problem is deciding how much to buy. One 12-bottle case will yield 72 5-ounce servings (a pretty full glass), but other variables must be considered: the number of guests and how old they are, if the event will be held indoors or outdoors, and if the weather will be warm or cool. Guests tend to drink more on Friday and Saturday nights than Sunday afternoon, and many hardly drink at all in warm weather. Caterers commonly figure on a three-to-one ratio of white wine to red wine consumption, but younger crowds are drinking more red wine than white these days.

In some states, your wine merchant can give you a refund or credit for an unused case, as long as it has not been refrigerated and is in perfect condition. In general, though, experienced professionals can make an excellent estimate of what you'll need. If a few bottles are left, they'll taste terrific in a few days, after the excitement has died down.

Chapter 14

Body and Soul

In which we remember why we drink wine

$\mathcal{B}$efore you rush out to buy a bottle of wine for dinner tonight, step back for a moment. A question remains: Why does wine attract us so strongly?

Because, in a disconnected world, wine connects. For thousands of years, human beings have known that wine was made to share. From the very beginning, it has linked us to each other and to the natural world.

Wine connects new acquaintances and re-connects old friends. It connects us to people we'll never meet, grapegrowers and winemakers far away. It connects us to harvests long past, sunlight long faded, rain long soaked into the earth. It connects us to wars, traditions, culture and history. It connects us to the time before history existed, when mountains and valleys took shape and the rocks emerged from below.

Most profoundly, wine connects us to ourselves. A winemaker and sage from Burgundy, Jacques Lardière, says that wine has fascinated human beings for millennia because it shows them something that they couldn't see any other way. "When you taste a wine, you realize that your response to it is unique to you," he says. "Through it you come to understand your own uniqueness as a person."

Wine offers a short respite from the noise of lives frantic with activities and obligations. Close your eyes, bend toward the glass and inhale the aroma of a wine. You'll find one tiny moment of quiet, when all distractions melt into pure sensation. "Wine nourishes us," says Lardière. "It links *le corps et le coeur*, body and soul."

No wonder wine brings us together and draws us back, again and again.

> *Wine, one sip of this will bathe the drooping spirits in delight beyond the bliss of dreams.*
> – John Milton

*In which you find sources for
lots of wine information, most of it free*

With just a little effort, you can be rolling in information about wine, wineries, wine regions and wine country tourism. Go for it!

Stuff for free

Winery newsletters

Call and ask to be added to the mailing lists of wineries whose wines you particularly like. Wineries often sell wines through their newsletters that cannot be obtained at retailers, such as older bottlings or special wines made in small quantities.

World Wide Web

The online world is saturated with wine information, chat groups, wine magazine sites and ratings listings. Many national wine institutes or tourist boards have useful sites detailing wine touring in their countries. Hundreds of wineries maintain Web sites which include announcements of new releases, tasting notes and lists of retailers carrying their wines.

Wine merchant newsletters

A great way to get a sense of a shop's personality. If you're looking for a local merchant you'll click with, call a few of them and ask for samples of their newsletters. It's a great way to learn about wines on sale in your area and to compare prices.

Kermit Lynch Wine Merchant newsletter

This Berkeley-based wine importer's monthly publication is a gem. Lynch spends much of each year traveling through France, buying the wines he likes best, no matter how obscure the regions or grape varieties. The newsletter will introduce you to his wonderful wine discoveries. (510-524-1524)

German Wine Information Bureau

A great source for well designed brochures and maps about German wines. They aren't sent directly to consumers, but wine merchants can obtain them through their German wine importers or distributors. One of the best items is a wine and food matching wheel which suggests German wines for everything from teriyaki steak to cheese and tomato pizza.

Buying wine online or by telephone

Direct shipping means that a merchant or winery sends wine directly to a consumer, often by-passing distributors in the state where the consumer lives. More and more wine lovers are taking advantage of direct shipping to obtain wines that they can't get from their local sources. However, liquor wholesalers and distributors, who have enjoyed monopolies as middlemen since Prohibition ended in 1933, are determined to end consumer access to alcohol through any channel other than the one they control. Their lobbyists have pushed restrictive laws through many state legislatures.

If you live in Florida, Georgia, Kentucky, North Carolina, Oklahoma, Indiana or Tennessee, your state's laws make it a felony to order wine from an out-of-state winery or merchant. In fact, if you live in any of the above states, even bringing wine home yourself from another state is a felony. Nineteen other states expressly prohibit direct shipping, though they have not made it a felony.

If you live in one of the 12 reciprocity states, you can order wine from merchants or wineries in any other reciprocity state. The states are California, Colorado, Idaho, Illinois, Iowa, Minnesota, Missouri, New Mexico, Oregon, Washington, West Virginia and Wisconsin.

For more information on the wholesalers' efforts to abolish direct shipping, contact Free the Grapes, *an advocacy group largely funded by the wine industry. The Web site includes up-to-date information on legal and legislative activities regarding direct shipping around the country. You can also ask to be notified if your state lawmakers are considering legislation affecting direct shipping, pro or con. (www.freethegrapes.org or 707-254-9292)*

To learn how your state regulates direct shipping, consult your local alcohol control agency or the Web site of the Wine Institute, a trade organization in California (www.wineinstitute.org).

If you live in a state where direct shipping is legal, you can buy wine from a host of merchants across the nation. Many merchants specialize in wines from particular regions or small producers. Look for their ads at the back of wine magazines

If you're hesitant about buying wine from a distance, surf over to California-based *Virtual Vineyards*. The site is so comprehensive that you'll feel confident about your choices, and you can get personalized help from a human being if you want it (www.virtualvin.com).

Take a look at Doug Frost's *Wine Society of the World,* a terrific Web site specializing in wines not available in the retail market, especially older wines. The bottlings come from all over the world and cover everything from Champagne to 100-year-old Madeira. Prices are way more reasonable than you'd imagine for some otherwise unobtainable treasures. A great place to find unique gifts (www.winesociety.com).

Books and publications

Dan Berger's Vintage Experiences, a weekly newsletter, is the written equivalent of having a casual conversation with a knowledgeable, candid and witty wine-business insider. Berger begins each issue with an opinionated commentary, then highlights a few wines he considers notable – and he never uses that darned 100-point rating scale. Many of the recommended wines are very reasonably priced. The two-page publication is faxed or mailed every Thursday, so readers have a fighting chance of finding Berger's recommended wines before they're sold out. ($52 per year for 48 issues, 888-662-9463.)

The University Wine Course, by Marian W. Baldy, Ph.D., is an excellent, comprehensive book covering wine from many different angles, including sensory analysis, grapegrowing and winemaking. If you're the kind of person who likes to work through a topic in depth, you'll love this. Every chapter has tests you can take to gauge your progress, and you'll also find precise instructions for setting up a number of interesting and valuable sensory evaluation exercises. ($35, Wine Appreciation Guild, 800-231-9463.)

The Oxford Companion to Wine, edited by Jancis Robinson, is precise, authoritative and crisply written. Like any encyclopedia, it contains lots of entries which are useful mostly to people who are trying to settle late-night bets in a bar, but it also answers just about any wine question. ($60, Oxford University Press)

A Wine and Food Guide to the Loire, by Jacqueline Friedrich, is much more specialized than the other books I've recommended, but worth reading for the author's take on wine and food in the context of this region and its people. She weaves in history, geology and personalities in a beautifully written volume. If you can read this without deciding to visit the Loire on your next trip to France, you've got more willpower than I do. ($27.50, Henry Holt)

Kellgren's Wine Book Catalog offers one of the best selections anywhere of books about wine, including general classics by writers like Hugh Johnson, travel guides to various wine regions and niche titles on subjects like trellising, wine chemistry and corkscrew collecting. If you haven't been able to find the book you're looking for anywhere else, chances are that you'll find it here. (800-274-4816 or www.wine-lovers-page.com/kellgren)

Wine Savvy: The Simple Guide to Buying and Enjoying Wine Anytime, Anywhere, by Heidi Yorkshire. This is my own book, so I'll let the reviewer from the *Wine Spectator* talk about it: "Yorkshire hits all the right notes in this simple little introduction to wine . . . This is a starter book [meant to] strip away the fear that accompanies a newcomer's confusion about such an apparently complicated subject." ($12.95, Duplex Media, 877-438-7539)

Not books, but useful

The only wine preservation product that really works is *Private Preserve*, a mix of gases that blankets wine remaining in the bottle to protect it from oxygen. It's an infinitely better method than those vacuum pump gizmos; compare the two and you'll see what I mean. A can of Private Preserve, which will treat dozens of bottles, costs $9.95 and is available at wine merchants and gourmet shops, or phone 707-252-4258 to order.

Get yourself a good corkscrew. The best is made by *Screwpull*, with a Teflon-coated worm that twists the cork out easily. The simplest model sells for about $20.

The Wine Aroma Wheel, Sparkling Wine Aroma Wheel and *Beer Flavor Wheel* (see Chapter 2) are sold by some wine and beer merchants, or can be ordered by sending a check for $6 per wheel to Dr. Ann Noble, Dept. of Viticulture and Enology, University of CA, Davis CA 95616.

Beringer Vineyards has adapted and simplified Noble's wheel into two versions, for white wines and red wines. A set of two wheels, plus instructions on setting up a simplified sensory seminar at home, are available for $3 in cash or check made out to Beringer Vineyards and sent to Beringer Vineyards Fulfillment Center, 615 Airpark Rd., Napa CA 94558. (Allow 4 to 6 weeks for delivery.)

The Tea Tasting

In which a wineless wine tasting is presented

Since this exercise was published in my previous book, *Wine Savvy*, I've heard from readers who say it's one of the most illuminating tasting experiences they've ever had. With ordinary black tea and a couple of other common kitchen ingredients, you can learn to recognize some of the basic building-blocks of wine: tannin, sweetness/fruitiness and acidity. Tea-tasting enthusiasts are not all beginners; I often hear from knowledgeable wine drinkers who say that the exercise has helped them clarify the basics.

This tea tasting is an adaptation of one devised by Tim Hanni, director of on-premise development for Beringer Wine Estates. When Hanni found himself trying to teach teetotaling waiters in a Georgia restaurant how to describe wines to customers, he had the brainstorm of using tea to illustrate his points.

The quantity below will be enough for two tasters. The "recipe" can be infinitely multiplied.

Ingredients

2-3 teabags of black tea (Lipton or similar)
4 teaspoons granulated sugar
fresh or bottled lemon juice
a tablespoon or two of heavy cream or half-and-half

Equipment for each taster

4 wine glasses
1 glass of water
1 paper cup (for spitting)
1 napkin

Before you start

1. Fill a 2-cup (16 ounce) measuring cup with boiling water and use all the teabags to brew very strong tea. Let it cool to room temperature.

2. Pour roughly equal amounts of tea into four glasses. Set the four glasses in a row, and think of them, from left to right, as 1, 2, 3, and 4. If you like, you can mark the base of each glass with the number, using a water-soluble marker. (It will wipe right off.)

3. Add 2 teaspoons of sugar each to glasses 2 and 3, and stir until the sugar dissolves.

Glass 1: Tannin

1. Take a mouthful from glass 1. Swish the tea around in your mouth before swallowing.

2. Now run your tongue over your teeth and along the roof of your mouth. What do you feel? If the tea was good and strong, you will probably feel a puckery, gritty, almost sandpapery sensation in your mouth, especially on your teeth. Your mouth could also feel dry, as if the moisture has been sucked out. You may also taste a bitterness on the back of your tongue.

Quite coincidentally, this exercise also provides practice in one of the wine lover's most important activities: spitting. Many people who are normally shy about spitting are quite happy to spit out the strong, bitter tea.

You've just experienced the distinctive taste and feeling of tannin. Tannin is present in strong tea, and it's also present in the skins, seeds and stems of wine grapes. When you bite into a grape with seeds, that gritty feeling between your teeth is tannin. In general, the longer the skins and seeds (and sometimes stems) of grapes remain in contact with grape juice that's being made into wine, the more tannin the wine will contain.

Glass 2: Sweetness

1. Take a mouthful from glass 2. Swish the tea around in your mouth before swallowing.

2. What do you taste first, the sweetness or the tannin? As you know, this glass of tea is the same strength as glass 1, but does it taste as strong or as tannic? Take another mouthful and pay attention to how the two elements — the sweetness and the tannin — interact. Does one overpower the other?

3. After you swallow, take note of the flavors that remain in your mouth. Is there any sort of aftertaste? How about other sensations?

Sweetness, or the impression of sweetness, is another key element in creating the taste of wine. Even though dry wines contain little or no sugar, the fact remains that some of them give an impression of sweetness, especially in the nose. Much of that impression is caused by hints of various fruit aromas in wine, such as grape, apple, pear, berry, cherry or even pineapple, to name just a few. (The aromas you smell are determined by many variables, especially the variety of grape from which the wine is made, the fermentation temperature, and the type of yeast used.) Overall, that impression is called fruitiness. Sensory researchers say that human beings interpret fruity aromas as "sweet" because they have learned to associate the aroma of fruit automatically with the taste of sweetness.

Other aromas in dry wine are not considered part of its fruitiness, but can also fool you into thinking the wine's sweet. If a wine is aged in oak barrels, it can pick up the scents of vanilla or clove, which most of us connect with sweet desserts. Some wines even have a buttery or butterscotch smell.

The next time a table wine seems sweet to you, spend a few moments trying to analyze its aromas. Then taste carefully. You may want to hold your nose so that you're not strongly swayed by the smells. You'll probably be able to confirm that the wine contains no sugar, or practically none. The "sweetness" that you're experiencing is the fruitiness of the nose instead, or other aromas that develop during the winemaking process.

Glass 3: Acidity

1. Squeeze a couple of teaspoons of lemon juice into glass 3. Stir to mix. Now, take a sip.

2. Does 3 taste as sweet as 2? They both contain the same amount of sugar. How has the addition of lemon changed the way you perceive the sweetness? How do the sweetness of the sugar and the acidity of the lemon interact?

Acidity is the third key element in the taste of wine. Acidity gives wines their zingy, fresh quality, and balances out sweetness or fruitiness with a refreshing crispness. Chances are, sample 3 didn't taste as sweet to you as 2, even though they both contain the same amount of sugar. The acid in the lemon juice has cut through the sweetness.

Often, when people complain that a wine is "too sweet," what they're really sensing is that it isn't crisp enough, that it doesn't have enough acidity to balance its fruity qualities. But too much acidity can make a wine taste sour and thin. Finding an equilibrium between sweetness and acidity is one of the winemaker's balancing acts.

Glass 4: Texture

1. Stir a good dollop of cream or half-and-half into glass 4. Take a sip and swirl it around in your mouth.

2. How does the cream change the taste of the tea? How does it change the way the tea feels in your mouth?

A liquid can create diverse physical sensations, such as smooth, creamy, sharp and rough. Some wines feel big and velvety, some are enjoyably prickly (sparkling wine is the best example), and some are thin and refreshing.

Of course, nobody puts dairy products in wine (although skim milk is sometimes used to clarify wine near the end of the winemaking process). But some wines undergo a second fermentation, called *malolactic fermentation*, which changes malic acid, a sharp-tasting acid found in grapes (and apples and rhubarb), to lactic acid, a mellower-tasting acid which is found in dairy products. Malolactic fermentation can be a factor in making a wine feel creamier in your mouth, as can *sur lie aging* (see page 52).

Pure tastes

Experiencing tannin, sweetness and acidity in a pure form gives you a good base for understanding why you do or don't like a certain wine.

For example, if you try a wine that feels rough or astringent in your mouth and leaves a bitter aftertaste, you'll realize that it has more tannin than you like. If a wine makes you pucker up, maybe it's too acidic for you; on the other hand, if it tastes rather flat but not sweet, perhaps it isn't acidic *enough*. And now you'll have a clue about how to differentiate between a wine that's actually sweet and one that's just fruity.

Acknowledgements

In which the author expresses her thanks

Many people around the world have been willing to share their enthusiasm for wine with me, and I am grateful to all. I would particularly like to recognize:

Joseph Anthony, my husband, partner and negotiator.

My parents, Analee and Boris Yorkshire, food and wine lovers and avid travelers whose adventures in distant lands have always inspired me. When they sent me on my first trip to Europe in 1971, they ignited a curiosity about the world that shaped my life. It was my father's stash of vintage Bordeaux that showed me what wonders could be found in a bottle.

John A. Rizzo and Donna Macdonald for their endless generosity and good humor, and all the photographs in *Simply Wine*.

Graphic designer Linda Wisner, Wisner Associates, and Jeannette Schilling for design that's both smart and beautiful.

Sandra Dorr, writing teacher and editor *par excellence*.

Cecil Chamberlin, M.D., sounding board, encouragement specialist and the best sort of wine connoisseur.

The indispensible Cheryl Russell.

Susan Sokol Blosser, friend and teacher.

Suzan Hall, who is unmatched at coming up with snappy book titles.

Mark Wigginton and Judy McDermott, my editors at the *Oregonian*, and all the *Oregonian* staff who have a hand in presenting my weekly column so beautifully.

The winemakers of Oregon, who showed me the glory of pinot noir.

Index

*H*eidi Yorkshire, wine and spirits columnist for the *Oregonian*, has written about wine, food and travel for *Bon Appétit* and other national magazines for more than a decade. A Certified Wine Educator, she teaches wine classes around the United States for corporate, consumer and trade audiences. One of her favorite presentations is "Pinot Noir 101," which she teaches each summer at the International Pinot Noir Celebration in McMinnville, Oregon. Heidi speaks French and Italian, and teaches seminars on French and Italian for food and wine lovers.

Her previous book, *Wine Savvy: The Simple Guide to Buying and Enjoying Wine Anytime, Anywhere*, was nominated for an IACP/Julia Child Cookbook Award. *Wine Savvy* was translated into Japanese and published in Japan by YoYoSha.

A native of Los Angeles, Heidi lived for several years in Paris and is now at home in Portland, Oregon. She is a longtime volunteer organizer for the Portland Farmers Market, founder of Summer Loaf, a festival of artisan bread, and an avid home cook and baker. She is also a student of Iyengar yoga.

Heidi lives with her husband, writer and tax specialist Joseph Anthony, and Bruiser, a Ragdoll cat.

Order Form

Ordered By

Name _____

Address _____

City _____ State ____ Zip _____

Daytime phone _____

(For use if problems arise in shipping your order.)

Shipping Address for Order

(if different from above)

Name _____

Address _____

City _____ State ____ Zip _____

Payment Method

❏ Check enclosed (Please make checks payable to Duplex Media.)

❏ MasterCard   ❏ VISA   ❏ Discover

Expiration date (required): _____/_____

Authorized signature: _____

Credit card #: _____

Order

Quantity

_____ Simply Wine @ $12.95 $ _____

_____ Wine Savvy @ $12.95 $ _____

                              Subtotal $ _____

                              Shipping $ _____

                              TOTAL $ _____

Shipping Costs

❏ Book Rate (can take up to 4 weeks for delivery):
   $2.50 for first book, $1 for each additional book

❏ Priority Mail: $4 for up to 4 books to same address

Contact Duplex Media

Call 503-335-3155 or toll-free 1-877-438-7539,
fax to 503-280-8964,
or mail to:
Duplex Media, P.O. Box 12081,
Portland OR 97212-0081